100% UNOFFICIAL!

OLYMPIC SPORT
THE WHOLE MUSCLE-FLEXING STORY

Glenn Murphy wrote his first book, *Why Is Snot Green?*, while working at the Science Museum, London. Since then he has written around twenty popular-science titles aimed at kids and teens, including the bestselling *How Loud Can You Burp?* and *Space: The Whole Whizz-Bang Story*.

These days he lives in sunny, leafy North Carolina – with his wife Heather, his son Sean and an *unfeasibly* large feline.

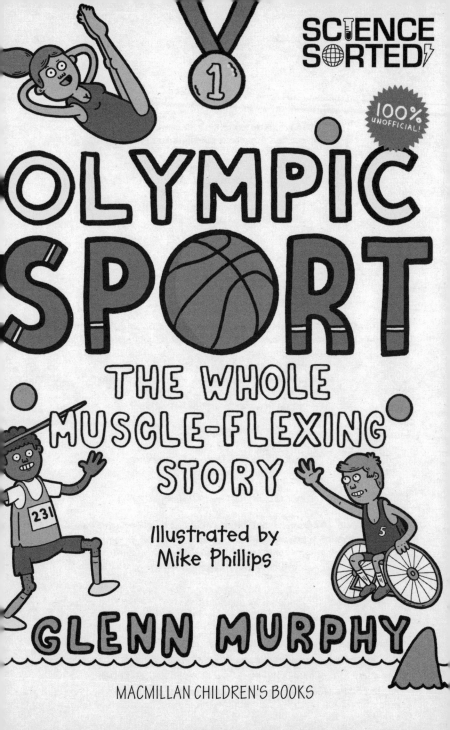

SCIENCE SORTED

1

100% UNOFFICIAL!

OLYMPIC SPORT

THE WHOLE MUSCLE-FLEXING STORY

Illustrated by
Mike Phillips

231

5

GLENN MURPHY

MACMILLAN CHILDREN'S BOOKS

Some material in this book has previous been published in 2012
by Macmillan Children's Books in *Does Farting Make You Faster?*

This edition published 2016 by Macmillan Children's Books
an imprint of Pan Macmillan
20 New Wharf Road, London N1 9RR
Associated companies throughout the world
www.panmacmillan.com

ISBN 978-1-4472-5468-3

Text copyright © Glenn Murphy 2012, 2016
Illustrations copyright © Mike Phillips 2012, 2016
Designed by Dan Newman

The right of Glenn Murphy and Mike Phillips to be identified as the author and illustrator of this work
has been asserted by them in accordance with the Copyright, Designs and Patents Act 1988.

1 3 5 7 9 8 6 4 2

A CIP catalogue record for this book is available from
the British Library.

Printed and bound by CPI Group (UK) Ltd, Croydon CR0 4YY

Picture credits: All photographs Shutterstock except for the following: page 34 Bettmann/
Getty Images; 43 ullstein bild/Getty Images; 50 Tony Duffy/Getty Images; 62 Steve Jennings/
Getty Images; 77 Greg Wood/Getty Images; 85 Christophe Simon/Getty Images;
129 Steve Babineau/Getty Images; 138 Mondadori Portfolio/Getty Images

CONTENTS

BIGGER, BETTER, FASTER, STRONGER

Are Olympic athletes born stronger and faster than the rest of us?

For the most part, no. All babies are born with more or less the same bone and muscle structures. It's not really the body you're born with that's important – it's what you do with it that counts. How big, strong or fast an athlete you become will depend mostly on how you feed and train your muscles, nerves and brain.

Is that really true?

For the most part, yes. Of course, if you suffer from a disease or growth problem, then your body may not develop quite as well, and it will be much tougher to reach the top levels of certain sports. Likewise, if you don't eat a healthy diet, or suffer from **malnutrition** (starvation or a lack of nutritious food) at a young age, then your muscles may never develop to their full size later on. But, all other things being equal, most healthy people should be able to reach Olympic levels of speed and strength with the right kind of training.

Where It All Started

The 2,700-year-old tradition of the **Olympic Games** began in **ancient Greece**. The first was held in the city of Olympia around 776 BC. In the earliest versions of the Games, the only events were footraces like **sprints** and **marathons**. But later came other events like boxing, wrestling, javelin and discus throwing.

Sporting (Dis)abilities

Until recently, it was often assumed that people with physical disabilities simply could not compete in top-level sports. But with modern training methods and technology, many disabled athletes are proving this idea false. South African sprinter **Oscar Pistorius** was born without the fibula (shin) bones in both legs, and at eleven months old had to have his legs removed from just below the knee and replaced with metal prostheses (or artificial limbs). By age thirteen, he was on the school rugby team, and went on to compete in tennis, wrestling and water polo tournaments. In 2004, he took up sprinting and, fitted with new, custom-designed carbon-fibre 'cheetah' legs, he went on to win three gold medals in the 100m, 200m and 400m events at the 2008 Paralympic Athletics World Championships. At the 2012 London Olympics he became the first amputee to compete against able-bodied athletes.

So with enough training I could run like an Olympic sprinter . . . jump like a high jumper . . . out–throw a shot putter?

Well, depending on your height, shape and body type, you may be better suited to some sports than others.

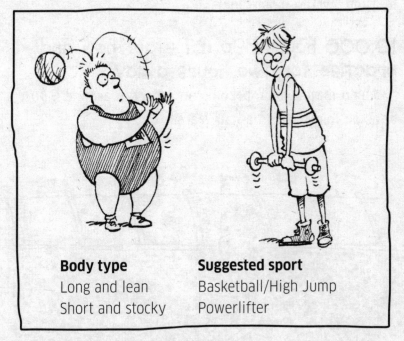

Body type	Suggested sport
Long and lean	Basketball/High Jump
Short and stocky	Powerlifter

That said, there aren't that many sports in which height or weight are necessarily a big advantage. And with enough time and practice you can become good (if not great) at more or less any sport. How far you eventually go will depend partly upon your natural shape, but mostly upon your **training**.

So how long would I have to train to be a top athlete?

Well, it varies from person to person, and from sport to sport, so it's hard to say. Some experts reckon that 10,000 hours of training is enough to take you from beginner to expert athlete. That seems to be the minimum for getting to a top level in most sports.

10,000 hours? So if I start now and practise for two hours a day . . .

. . . then maybe you'll become an expert in around 5,000 days, or thirteen and a half years.

Nearly fourteen years?

Yep. Of course, you can become very good at your favourite sport with a lot less. A little sports training each week is much better than none at all, and will still make you stronger, faster, healthier and more skilled.

Most professional athletes train for several hours a day, six days a week. So, if you want to be an **Olympic champion** by the time you're twenty-five with just two hours of training a day, you need to start at age eleven!

Yikes. Better get to it, then!

No time like the present . . .

Does your body have bits especially for doing sports?

Well, no – not quite. Your body has systems for doing lots of different things, including keeping you upright, keeping you well fed and keeping you aware of your surroundings. None of these systems developed especially for doing sports. But a couple, like the musculoskeletal and nervous systems, are particularly handy for learning the physical skills needed for modern sports.

Born to Run

Our brain and bodies evolved the ability to jump and throw, not to leap over high bars or throw javelins in sporting competitions, but because physical abilities like this helped our ancestors survive. Having a well-developed musculoskeletal and nervous system was particularly important for high-energy, physical activities like running, hunting and fighting. Later on, we turned these highly developed systems to other things.

So what are these systems made of?

As you probably know from biology, at its most basic level, your body is made of **cells**. There are over 300 different types of cells, which do lots of different jobs within the body. These include red blood cells, which carry oxygen around the body; **nerve cells**, which carry messages to, from and within the brain; and **skin cells**, which help protect your body from scrapes, sunburn and nasty bacteria.

RED BLOOD CELL

OK, I get all that . . .

Now many of these cells are also organized into **tissues**. Tissues are sheets or clusters of cells that work together to perform a certain task. Again, there are lots of tissue types in the body, including **muscle tissue** (used to build your muscles), **nervous tissue** (used to build your nerves and brain) and **epithelial tissue** (used to build your skin and the lining of your gut). Most tissues contain two or more different types of cell.

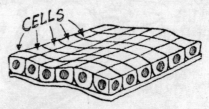

CELLS

EPITHELIAL TISSUE

Sounds simple enough.

Right. But it doesn't stop there. Tissues, in turn, are organized into organs. Just as a tissue contains two or more different cell types, an organ contains two or more types of tissue (and many, many cell types), all working together.

Some organs do one job, while others do several at once. The **heart**, for example, is basically just a pump keeping blood moving around the body. The **liver**, on the other hand, does lots of different things, including filtering poisons and toxins, adding or removing sugar to your bloodstream, helping you digest fats and proteins, and much, much more.

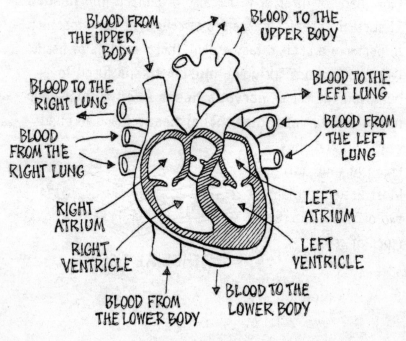

BLOOD FROM THE UPPER BODY

BLOOD TO THE UPPER BODY

BLOOD TO THE RIGHT LUNG

BLOOD TO THE LEFT LUNG

BLOOD FROM THE RIGHT LUNG

BLOOD FROM THE LEFT LUNG

RIGHT ATRIUM

LEFT ATRIUM

RIGHT VENTRICLE

LEFT VENTRICLE

BLOOD FROM THE LOWER BODY

BLOOD TO THE LOWER BODY

So organs are pretty important, then.

Right. They're also pretty tough to replace if they become damaged or diseased. Which is why **organ transplants** (like heart, lung or kidney transplants) are such a serious business.

And it won't surprise you to learn that even your organs are, well . . .

Organized?

Exactly. Organs work together in **organ systems**. All of them are important for the practice of sports and other physical activities, but perhaps the most important of these (for sports at least) is the one that moves you about: the **musculoskeletal** system.

So how does that work?

Thought you'd never ask. Read on and let's find out . . .

Organ Systems

cardiovascular system	heart, veins, arteries and smaller blood vessels
digestive system	teeth, stomach, liver and intestines
excretory system	kidneys and bladder
nervous system	brain, spinal cord and nerves
musculoskeletal system	bones, muscles, ligaments and tendons

Does farting make you run faster?

Sadly, no. **Strong muscles** and **peak fitness** make you run faster, but turbocharged bottom burps will have little effect on your sprinting speed. Instead, track athletes have highly developed muscles that are built and trained for running, and powerful body systems that deliver oxygen to their muscles at a faster rate.

You're telling me farting doesn't help at all?

Not as far as I know, no. (Although I must admit I'm not

sure how hard sports scientists have tried to study that.)
According to the experts, it's not **fart power** that speeds
up a sprinter – it's **muscle power**.

So sprinters have more muscles than normal people? Like extra leg muscles or something?

Not exactly, no. Athletes have the same number of bones
and muscles as everybody else. The difference is that
champion athletes train their musculoskeletal systems to
grow and work in different ways.

So athletes have the same number of muscles – they're just bigger and stronger?

Well, trained athletes do tend to have bigger, stronger
muscles than your average non-sporty slob. But it's
not just the size and strength of your muscles that's
important. Female gymnasts, for example, are enormously
strong. But they often have long, flat muscles that seem
puny at first glance.

So a strong athlete may have bigger muscles than most
people. Or they may have muscles that are longer, contain
more muscle fibres or use energy and oxygen more
efficiently. Through training, athletes may also gain more
control over individual muscles, meaning that they can
contract them harder than the average person can.

Wait – so athletes can do things with their muscles that we can't?

Sometimes, yes. As we'll see in later chapters, through training, athletes can learn to control their musculoskeletal systems to perform feats of strength, speed and agility that seem almost ... well ... **superhuman**.

Depending on how you count them, the human body contains between 206 and 250 bones, and between 640 and 850 muscles.

Howzat, then?

Let's start with your standard bone-and-muscle set-up.

a couple of hundred bones
(arranged into a skeleton)

+

hundreds more muscles,
ligaments and tendons

=

musculoskeletal system

The whole lot is wrapped in a
covering of fleshy bags and straps
called connective tissue or fascia
(pronounced 'fash-ee-ah').

Eh?
What's all that for?

It's for keeping you up.
And moving you about.

But I thought your skeleton held you up. And the muscles attached to the bones move you about. You move the muscles, and the muscles pull on the bones, right?

Ah, but that's not quite the whole story. In school textbooks, you're usually shown a skeleton, and told that the hard bones give your body its shape and strength. Then the whole lot gets pulled around by stringy muscles attached to the ends of the bones. But in reality it doesn't work exactly that.

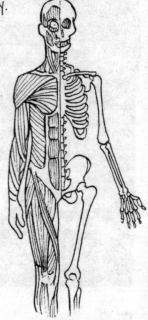

For starters, muscles don't actually attach to bones anywhere in the body. **Ligaments** – small, fleshy strings that don't stretch or contract very much – attach to the ends of the bones and keep them all wired together. But **muscles**, along with their less stretchy cousins **tendons**, don't attach directly to bones at all. Instead, they attach to fleshy bags of **fascia** that surround every bone and every joint in your body. More layers of fascia lie outside the muscles too, wrapping round them in spiralling straps and sheets.

In fact, rather than think of a skeleton with layers of muscle, tendon and fascia on top, it's better to think of the body as a big **fleshy suit of armour**. The armour is made of fascia, and has its own strong structure. The bones and muscles float within this big suit of armour, locked in place by ligaments and tendons.

Ligament means 'joining thing'.

So your bones and muscles aren't the only things holding you up?

Right. Or the only things moving you around.

Bones, ligaments, tendons and fascia all give structure to the body. Together, they form **chains of pressure** around the limbs and the trunk of the body, which hold it up. But they also move you around, as the muscles within these chains change shape.

Get It Sorted – Working Muscles

Muscles, often arranged in pairs (or threes, or fours) on opposite sides of the same limb or body part, move body parts in opposing directions. For example, shortening (or **contracting**) the **bicep muscle** (on the front of your upper arm) bends your elbow, while contracting your **tricep** (on the back of your upper arm) straightens the elbow. But these muscles aren't really pulling on the arm bones to make them move. Instead, contracting your bicep muscle makes it shrink, which pulls the whole, fleshy, bony structure of the lower arm upward. The muscles pull on the tendons, the tendons on the fascia, the fascia on the bones, and the bones on everything that surrounds them.

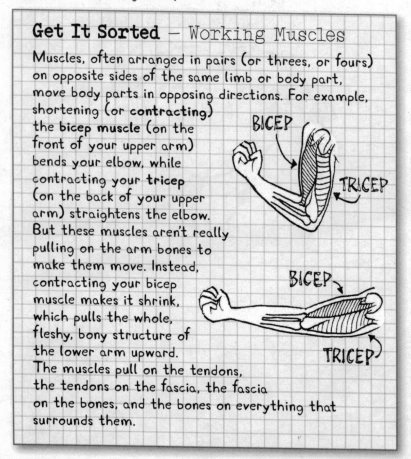

BICEP

TRICEP

BICEP

TRICEP

OK, so muscles work together with all the other stuff to move us around. So why is that important to athletes?

Because, when they train and exercise, athletes aren't just reshaping their muscles. It's true that an athlete's muscles may become longer, stronger and more efficient than those of the average person (we'll see more about how this happens later on). But, just as importantly, athletes also reshape their tendons, fascia – even their bones – to adjust to new, powerful and sporty movements.

So it's not that top athletes have more muscles than everyday people – they have the same number of muscles as everybody else. It's what's inside them – and all around them – that's different.

OK . . . so how different can they get?

Let's find out . . .

IN THE OLYMPIC STADIUM

Sprinting

Could the world's fastest sprinter beat a cheetah?

Not a chance. A cheetah can hit around 70mph (112km/h), which makes them more than twice as speedy as the world's fastest human sprinters, who have yet to top 28mph (45km/h). Even your pet cat could beat that.

What?! My cat could outrun an Olympic sprinter?! No way!

Yep. I'm afraid so. The average moggy can easily hit 30 mph (48km/h) at a full sprint. This makes them a little faster than 100m-sprint world-record holder **Usain Bolt**, whose fastest speed in his record-breaking 2009 race was just under 27.8mph (45km/h).

Bigger cats, like lions and leopards, can sprint at over 50mph (80km/h) and would leave all human sprinters in the dust.

As for racing a cheetah – forget about it. In 2009, Usain Bolt made history by running the 100m sprint in just 9.58 seconds. In theory, a cheetah could do it in less than four seconds.

In tests, even lazy cheetahs, coaxed into chasing stuffed toys (dragged from cars by curious scientists), have run 100m in under 6.5 seconds.

By the time Usain Bolt hit the finish line, the cheetah would already be sitting there, licking its paws.

Are cats especially fast sprinters, then?

Cats are fast, but not uniquely so. As a matter of fact, though, plenty of mammals can outrun us over short distances, including **warthogs** (30mph), **grizzly bears** (30mph) and **giraffes** (32mph). Which just goes to show . . .

. . . that you should never try to outrun a grizzly bear?

Well, yes. But, also, humans aren't really built for sprinting. We're very good at long-distance running (more about that later). And some of us are much faster than others. But, compared to other mammals, we have a pretty feeble top speed.

Why is that?

It's partly to do with how our muscles are built, or, more specifically, the type and number of **muscle fibres** within them.

Muscle fibres are tiny, fleshy threads that are bundled togethe to create whole muscles like the biceps or triceps. Now here's the tricky bit. There are two kinds of skeletal muscle fibre: **type I** (or **slow-twitch**) and **type II** (**fast-twitch**).

There are two other types of muscle in the human body – smooth muscle (which covers and lines the internal organs) and cardiac muscle (found only in the heart).

22

Most human muscles contain both types of fibres, and
the amount of fast-twitch fibres in muscles varies. But, in
Olympic sprinters, up to 80% of the leg and hip muscles
consist of type II (fast-twitch) fibres. This is part of what
makes Usain Bolt way faster than average. Elite sprinters
train to increase the amount of fast-twitch fibres in their
muscles.

So they can be more like cheetahs?

Something like that, yes. In a cheetah, it's more like 82%
fast-twitch muscle. This may not seem like that much
more. But combined with the cheetah's longer, four-
legged stride (and some other neat tricks it has for
sprinting), this makes the cheetah, in turn, more than
twice as fast as Usain Bolt.

Do you think, one day, a human sprinter will come along who can outrun a cheetah?

It seems unlikely. Experts reckon that even with as much fast-twitch muscle as possible, human beings are incapable of reaching more than 30 to 35mph. With the right diet and training, you can alter your muscle structure, increase your running speed by 50% or more and maybe even become an Olympic champion. But, no matter what-a you eat-a . . .

Animals that Can Out-sprint Humans

Top Speed (mph)	27.8	30	32
Animal	human (Usain Bolt)	warthog, grizzly bear, kangaroo, domestic cat	reindeer, gira

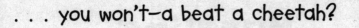

. . . you won't—a beat a cheetah?

Exactly.

I'm going to write that on my running vest.

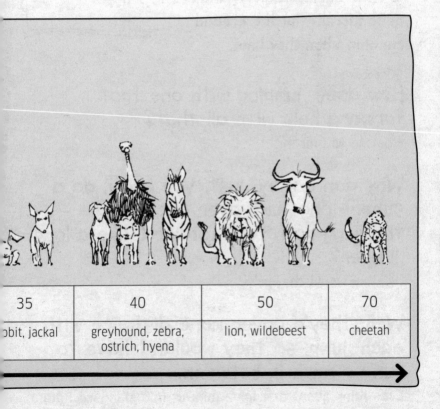

| 35 | 40 | 50 | 70 |
| bit, jackal | greyhound, zebra, ostrich, hyena | lion, wildebeest | cheetah |

Hurdling

Why do hurdlers do the splits when they jump?

Unlike long jumpers, hurdlers try not to spend too much time in the air. Their split-legged leaps allow them to clear hurdles quickly and, quite literally, hit the ground running when they land.

How does jumping with one foot forward help with all that?

What do you mean?

Why don't they just, you know, do a super-long jump over each hurdle – throwing both feet forward, like a long-jumper?

OK, how would that help?

Well, they'd cover more distance with each jump, so they wouldn't have to run so much in between.

Let's think about that for a minute. In a standard 110m

hurdles race, the runners have to cover the distance as quickly as possible, clearing ten hip-height hurdles along the way. Agreed?

Agreed.

Now which do you think takes more effort – leaping a 1.2m hurdle, or running a few metres along the flat track?

Dunno.

Let me put it this way. Which would you rather do: run once round an athletics track, or work your way round the same track in a series of non-stop hip-height leaps, one right after another?

Yikes. I'd rather run. I don't know if I'd even make it once round the track doing non-stop jumps like that.

Me neither.

Now, what if I asked you to race a friend round the same track, only you're allowed to run the whole way, while your friend has to do the non-stop, bounding leaps we talked about before. Who do you think would cross the finish line first?

Leaping vs Running

The difference between running and hurdling is like the difference between driving a car (horizontal movement) and launching a rocket (vertical movement). It takes less force to shift your weight one metre horizontally along the track than it does to shift it one metre vertically, or straight up. So while sprinting requires powerful contractions of your thigh and calf muscles, one leg right after the other, hurdling requires generating a large amount of force with your jumping leg to overcome the effects of gravity pulling down on your body. Tough as it is, sprinting takes less energy.

Wait – is my friend a kangaroo?

Err . . . no. Your friend is human. Like you.

Oh. OK. In that case, it's just stupid. I would win easily, because it wouldn't be a fair race.

Why not?

Because running is much faster than – ohhhhhhhh, now I get it . . .

Exactly. The runner would cover the same ground much faster than the jumper. That's because the more time you spend in the air, the less time you can spend **accelerating**.

Runners accelerate (or speed up) a little bit every time a foot pushes off the ground. But, the second the foot leaves the ground and stops pushing, **drag** – caused by **air resistance** – starts to slow the runner down in mid-air.

Sprinters maintain top speed by taking lots of short, rapid strides, spending as little time 'in the air' as possible, to avoid losing speed. Hurdlers try their best to do the same.

All that leaping must take a lot of training.

Yep, in fact, top hurdlers spend almost as much time perfecting their leaping technique as they do exercising and running. Like sprinters, hurdlers train hard to build lots of fast-twitch muscle fibre in their leg muscles. But they also stretch the muscles and tendons of their legs to make them more flexible, and do special **plyometric exercises** to build explosive power for leaping.

Give it a go!

If you want to add rocket-like leaping power to your legs, try out this exercise.

Exercise:	jump squat
Type:	plyometric
Goal:	leg strength, explosive power for leaping and jumping

Start standing, both feet flat on the ground, hip-width apart. Place your hands either side of your head, palms facing forward, fingers to temples. Keeping your back straight, quickly squat down, lowering your hips to your heels immediately. Push back up, straightening both legs and launching yourself off the ground in a standing position. Land toes first, and repeat.

Try to do as many as you can in one minute.
Here's what you should aim for:

up to 10/min	beginner
10–20/min	intermediate
20–30/min	athlete
30–50/min	champion

Jumps and Pole Vaulting

What's the highest, and furthest, a human has ever jumped?

As of 2012, the highest an athlete has ever jumped in a sporting competition is 2.45m. The longest jump, a record dating way back to 1991, is 8.95m.

Under 2.5m? Is that it? That doesn't seem so high.

Why do you say that?

Well, since most high jumpers are over six feet tall, about two metres, anyway, that means they only have to jump half a metre, doesn't it?

If all they had to do was touch the bar with their heads, then yes. But in a high-jump event, you have to get your whole body over the bar – head, hips, feet, the lot. Imagine a brick wall, the top of which is at least a metre higher than your own head. Now imagine trying to jump right over it, in one go, without grabbing (or even touching) the top.

Oh. I didn't think of it like that.

Yep. And champion high-jump athletes do that every day.

So why do they jump over it backwards, then? That's always seemed a bit silly to me.

It's the most efficient way anyone has ever found (at least so far) of lifting your **centre of gravity** (hips), along with the head, feet and everything else, over the greatest possible height. That's why Olympic high jumpers still use it today to break records, clearing heights of 2.4m or more.

The Fosbury Flop

The modern high jumper's backward-flopping leap is called the **Fosbury Flop**, named after American high jumper **Dick Fosbury**. He invented the technique in 1963, when he was just sixteen years old. He used it to win a gold medal for America in the 1968 Olympic Games – setting a new world record with a jump of 2.24m. Within ten years, every Olympic athlete was jumping that way.

In a Fosbury Flop, the athlete leaps backwards, leading with the back of the head, and arches his/her body over the bar. First the head, then the shoulder blades, hips, backs of the knees and finally the heels clear the bar one by one. The jumper lands flat on his/her back, usually finishing with a backwards roll as the legs continue swinging over the face.

'I didn't train to make the Olympic team until 1968. I simply trained for the moment. I never even imagined I would be an Olympic athlete. It always seemed to evolve.'

Dick Fosbury, Olympic high jumper, gold medallist, and President of the World Olympians Association

34

So jumping backwards turned out to be the best way. That's pretty crazy.

Yep.

What about long jumpers, then? Why do they jump feet first, rather than head first? Is that so they can jump higher too?

Well, yes and no. Long jumpers are basically sprinters who try to keep as much of their horizontal footspeed and momentum as possible during a last-minute leap into the air. Once they've left the ground, throwing both feet forward helps to keep their centre of gravity moving along, rather than upward. Some long jumpers also continue their 'run' in mid-air, with a cycling motion of the legs. This, too, helps keep their weight moving forward.

Reaching out with the feet also helps prevent the jumper from falling backwards into the sand at the end of the jump. Since the total jump distance is measured to the rearmost 'dent' they leave in the sand, falling back after a jump is a catastrophic mistake.

Using this feet-first-flying method, male long jumpers have cleared distances of almost **9m**, while triple jumpers have managed an impressive **18.3m**.

Whoa!

Even Longer Jumpers

In triple jump, the take-off board from which the jump is measured is set 12m further back from the landing pit than in the long jump. It's from here that the triple jumper begins his first leap, making two more leaping, bounding steps before leaving the ground for the last time, sailing through the air and landing in the sandpit. Since they count the bit where they're hopping and skipping as part of the jump, triple jumpers naturally cover more ground than long jumpers.

Give it a go!

If you want to add some length to your own jumps, try these simple exercises. Practice makes perfect!

Exercise: standing long jump
Type: plyometric/skill
Goal: explosive power, coordination

1. Stand at a marked point on the ground or grass, with both feet flat on the ground, hip-width apart. Start with your arms held straight behind you.

2. Bend your knees, swing your arms forward and jump as far as you can along the ground landing on the balls of both feet, with good balance.

3. Turn round, and see if you can jump back on to your original take-off spot.

4. Turn round and repeat the jump – this time trying to beat your previous record. Use a tape measure to record your personal best each week.

5. Find a couple of friends, and stage a standing jump competition.

The world record for a standing long jump is **3.71m**. Good luck!

How do you learn to pole vault (without seriously injuring yourself)?

Pole vaulting is probably the most difficult to learn of all the athletic field skills. To do it well, you need great strength, timing and coordination. But you learn to do it the same way you learn any other physical skill: little by little, by trial and error, until your brain and body commit the movement to memory.

I'm not surprised it's the most difficult. I mean, pole vaulting looks hard.

Yep. No two ways about it: pole vaulting is hard.

Learning any physical skill as complex as pole vaulting takes a bit of knowledge, a lot of coaching, tons of practice and the formation of something called muscle memory.

Once a skill has been performed, corrected and repeated enough times, your body learns how to do it without thinking, and it'll remember how to do it for many years afterwards.

Pole Vaulting Step by Step

To pull off a successful pole vault, you have to do all the following things, and all with perfect timing:

1. **Run** at close to full speed, carrying a pole up to 5m long over your head.

2. Without stopping, **plant** the tip of the pole precisely into a box just 15cm wide and 20cm deep.

3. **Leap** into the air, **hang on** to the pole as it bends almost in two, and **swing your legs** towards the sky until you're in a perfect upside-down handstand on the end of the upright pole.

4. **Flip** your whole body over the high bar without knocking into it (or letting your pole knock into it).

5. **Fall** feet first 5-6m, back to earth, landing squarely on the crash mat without hurting yourself.

All skills that enter your muscle memory are like this. Remember when you first learned to ride a bike?

Yeah. That was hard too.

Right. It was tricky at first, but with enough practice you could do it if you concentrated on pedalling steadily, keeping your balance and not falling off. But after a bit more practice you didn't need to think about pedalling or balancing at all. The bike-riding skill entered your muscle memory, and you gained the ability to ride a bike without thinking.

That's all very well, but it's not quite the same with pole vaulting, is it?

Why's that?

I mean, if you fall off a bike, you just topple to the ground. If you fall off a pole in mid-vault, you could end up falling five metres on to your head!

Very true.

So how do you learn to do something that difficult and dangerous without crippling yourself or cracking your head open or something?!

You take it a little at a time, making sure your body is happy with each 'baby step' along the way.

40

Pole Vaulting 'Baby Steps'

Here's how most beginners build up to a full pole vault in ten small, safe steps.

1. Practise **jogging** and **running** with the pole over your head.

2. Practise **dipping** the end of the pole towards the ground as you run.

3. Practise small **leaps** off the ground, right after the tip of the pole touches the ground.

4. Practise **planting** the pole into the pole box in mid-jog, but don't jump.

5. Hold the pole halfway down (to limit the height), then practise **mini-vaults**. To do these, you jog at the box, plant the pole, make a small jump and hang on to the pole (head up, feet down) as you ride it the short distance to the crash mat, landing feet first.

6. Repeat the mini-vault, this time **lifting both feet** to make an L-shape, so that you cling to the pole in a seated position, landing on your bottom.

7. Repeat, but this time **swing your feet higher**, pointing them towards the sky. Land on your back.

8. Repeat, swinging your feet up and extending your hips and arms until you're fully **inverted** (upside down). Turn in the air and land chest down, facing back the way you came.

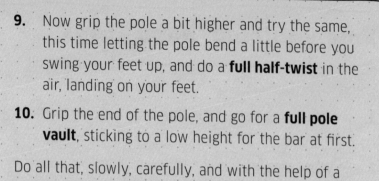

9. Now grip the pole a bit higher and try the same, this time letting the pole bend a little before you swing your feet up, and do a **full half-twist** in the air, landing on your feet.

10. Grip the end of the pole, and go for a **full pole vault**, sticking to a low height for the bar at first.

Do all that, slowly, carefully, and with the help of a qualified coach, and you'll be doing your first proper pole vault within weeks. Then it takes many more months (or years) to get really good at it.

It still seems like a lot of hard work.
Well, you could always take up long jump instead. Or move to Eastern Europe.

How would that help?
I hear they're very good at pole vaulting in Pole-land!

— **Groan . . .**

Heheheheh.

'You need to work very hard; you have to spend a lot of time practising your sport – six to seven hours daily.'

Sergey Bubka, Olympic pole-vault gold medallist, who broke the world record for pole vaulting 35 times

Javelin, Discus, Shot Put and Hammer Throws

Has anyone ever lobbed a discus right out of a stadium? According to legend, the Greek hero Heracles once did this in

one of the first ever Olympic Games. But in reality the discus thrown in modern athletic events is too heavy to be thrown that far.

Come on, how hard could it be? I lobbed a frisbee right out of our local park once. And I'm no Olympic athlete.

OK . . . but frisbees are usually made of plastic, and they're very light. Most only weigh 200g or less. A discus weighs between **1 and 2kg**, or about the weight of a good-sized bag of potatoes. They're made of heavy rubber and metal, and they're about the same size as a small dinner plate, only much thicker in the middle. But imagine hurling the bag of potatoes – rather than the dinner plate – and you'll have a better idea of how far it's likely to go.

Yeah, I doubt I could've thrown those spuds over the trees, right enough. So what about javelins, hammers and stuff?

At between **600g and 800g**, an Olympic **javelin** weighs about the same as a discus. The solid-metal **hammers** and **shots** used in hammer throw and shot put are quite a bit heavier, weighing up to 7.2kg.

Get It Sorted – Hammers and Shot

The shot is a solid metal ball, usually made of iron and steel. It gets its name from the weighty **cannonballs** (also known as **iron shots**) that were thrown in older versions of the event. 'Shot putting', then, is literally putting the shot as far away from yourself as possible in a single toss.

The **hammer** is a metal ball on the end of a long metal chain with a handle at one end for swinging. Ancient **hammer-throwing** events used to be just that – throwing large, heavy blacksmith's hammers.

At some point, the objects used for the official games changed, but the names stuck.

Is it just the biggest and strongest athletes who throw the furthest?

Not necessarily. Just because an athlete is big and muscly doesn't mean he's stronger than his smaller rivals. And, even if he is strong, that doesn't automatically mean he has the explosive strength and technique needed for a world-class throw.

What do you mean?

Well, we've already learned that **explosive power** comes from **quick-firing (fast-twitch) muscle fibres**, and that success in sprinting and jumping requires plenty of these fibres in the muscles of the legs and hips, right?

Right.

Well, throwing a javelin, discus or shot put requires massive amounts of explosive power too. This comes from exercising the muscles of the upper body (the arms, chest and back, in particular) in ways that increase the number of **fast-twitch fibres** within.

You can make your muscles grow bigger by lifting heavy weights very slowly (weightlifters do this all the time). When you do this, you're actually making tiny rips in your muscle fibres. Later, as you rest and recover  from training, your body repairs your torn muscle fibres, just in case you try the same thing again. As a result, your muscles grow stronger. But this type of slow strength training won't necessarily make you better at throwing a javelin or shot.

Why not?

Well, just because you can lift a 100kg object off the ground doesn't mean you can throw it (you'd almost certainly injure yourself trying). If you want the sort of power you need for Olympic throwing events you have to build muscles that can contract harder and faster, giving more explosive bursts of power to your arms, legs and core muscles.

So how do you do that?

You start by lifting weights slowly to build your muscles to increase your **maximal strength**, then continue by using special types of exercise to convert that maximal strength into explosive power. For the most part, this means using something called plyometrics.

In plyometric exercise, you begin by lengthening a muscle, then force it to contract hard and fast, then immediately force it to stretch out again, and repeat. You can do this using weights, or with bodyweight exercises like the **plyometric press-up** (see page 51 if you want to give it a go yourself).

As with all muscle-building exercise, this creates miniature snaps and tears in your muscle fibres, which grow back stronger as they heal. But it also encourages the growth of **fast-twitch muscle fibres**, specifically, which grow back much thicker and stronger than they were before.

In practice, most throwers do end up pretty huge. They tend to have very large chest, arm and back muscles, and develop huge maximum and explosive strength.

OK, so now you're super-strong, and you have crazy exploding chest muscles. Now you're ready to win the gold medal for discus?

Nope. Not by a long shot.

What? Why not?

Because to be good at the throwing events, you have to study and practise correct **throwing technique**. After all, it's no use being ultra-strong and having all that explosive muscle-power if you end up tossing a discus or hammer in the wrong direction.

Whoa. That sounds kind of dangerous.

Wildly thrown hammers do still injure people from time to time. In the past, quite a few people (mostly coaches and trainers standing close to the thrower) have even been killed this way.

Yikes!

But nowadays the **throwing circle** used in the hammer-throw event is surrounded by a **tall, C-shaped cage**, which protects the coaches and crowds alike.

That's a relief. In that case, I might actually watch it some time.

Well, it's always safe if you're watching it on TV.

'It took me time to realize that the men who won Olympic gold medals in the decathlon are just men, just like me.'

Dan O'Brien, Olympic decathlete and gold medallist

Give it a go!

Exercise: press-up
Type: plyometric
Goal: arm strength, explosive power for throwing

1. Start by lying face down on the ground, palms either side of your chest.

2. Keeping your back and legs straight, you're going to push down hard with your hands, straightening your elbows and launching your body off the ground. Throughout this movement, you should stay straight from the backs of your heels to the back of your neck, as if you have a long plank attached to your spine and the backs of your legs.

3. For a standard press-up, all you have to do is straighten your elbows. But for a plyometric press-up you have to push hard enough to lift your hands right off the ground, so that you're lifted – straight-backed and straight-armed – into the air. Clap your hands together while you're in the air.

4. As you drop back down, let your elbows bend to absorb and slow your fall, lowering your chest to within a few centimetres of the ground.

5. Repeat.

Try to do as many as you can in a minute. Here's what you should aim for:

up to 10/min	beginner
10–20/min	intermediate
20–30/min	athlete
30–50/min	superathlete

Get It Sorted – Decathlon, Heptathlon and Pentathlon

Decathlon

A multi-event athletic competition in which athletes compete in ten different track and field events over two days, adding the scores from each in order to decide the overall winner. Olympic decathlon events include almost every type of athletic track and field event, including **high jump, long jump, shot put, javelin, discus, pole vault,** two types of **sprint, hurdles** and a **middle-distance race.**

Heptathlon

A multi-event athletic competition in which female athletes compete in seven different track and field events. Basically, it's a decathlon without the discus, pole vault or 100m-sprint events. Again, scores from each event are totalled in order to decide the overall winner.

Modern Pentathlon

A multi-sport competition in which male or female athletes compete in five different events - most quite different from those seen in the decathlon and heptathlon. The Olympic modern pentathlon features a 200m **swim**, **horse jumping**, a 3km cross-country **run**, **pistol shooting** and **fencing**!

The rules of the modern penthalon state that the winner is the athlete with the most points at the end of all five events.

Players

Multi-event athletes compete individually, taking turns or facing opponents head-to-head in each event.

Equipment

Multi-event athletes use the same equipment - shoes, javelins, poles, trunks, swords, pistols, and so on - as the competitors in the individual track and field events.

Give it a go!

Exercise: stage your own heptathlon
Type: skill
Goal: skill, coordination

1. Find a wide, open space with plenty of room to run, jump and throw (and no one to injure).

2. Grab two or more friends, three heavy beanbags, three long bamboo sticks, three frisbees, a long spool of ribbon, some masking tape and a pad and pencil.

3. (Optional) Make three medals: one bronze, one silver and one gold, using a 2p piece, a 50p piece, and a £1 coin. Clip a small bulldog clip on to each one, then thread a piece of ribbon through and tie the ends to make a wide loop, big enough to go over your head.

4. Write the list of events in a column down the left-hand side of the notepad page, then write the competitors' names in a row across the top. This is your scoring grid. The events are: sprint, long jump, triple jump, shot put, javelin, discus and marathon.

5. Start with event number one – the sprint. Choose a starting point and mark out a line using two beanbags and a length of ribbon on the ground. Now mark out a finish line about 100m away. (If you can find two trees within four metres of each other, tape

the ribbon at chest height between them, then work backwards from there to mark out a starting line.) Line the players up, then, all together, say 'Ready, set, GO' and make a dash for the finish. Note the winner on the notepad.

6. Now move on to event number two – the standing long jump. Go back to your sprint starting line, stand behind it, then one at a time leap as far as you can, landing feet-first. Have one of the other players watch and mark the spot where you landed with a beanbag. Leave it there while the next player jumps, marking his/her jump with the second beanbag. Then repeat for the remaining player(s). Each player gets three attempts. If you jump further than your previous beanbag marker, you can shift it forward to indicate your new record. At the end of all the jumps, the player with the beanbag furthest from the start line wins. Note the winner.

7. Now pick up the beanbags and move back to the starting line for event number three – the triple jump. This is almost the same as the standing jump, except that you (a) get to take a run-up, (b) have to hop or skip twice before reaching the starting (take-off) line and (c) have to take off from one foot instead of two. Mark your jump with a beanbag as before. Everyone gets three attempts each. At the end, note the winner.

8. Event number four is the standing beanbag shot put. For this, each player crouches behind the starting line with a beanbag held in one hand, just beneath one ear. To throw, stand, twist your body and launch the beanbag as far as you can, pushing upward and outward with your palm (no overarm throws). Leave the beanbag where it lands while the other players throw theirs. At the end of the round, mark the beanbag landing spots with a short strip of masking tape (you can write the players' initials on it with the pencil), then proceed to round two. As with the jumps, each player gets three attempts. The longest throw after three rounds wins. Note the winner.

9. Event number five is the foam javelin. Use the starting line as your take-off point, then follow the instructions above to play the event. Again, you can mark the landing points with masking tape between rounds. The longest throw wins. Note the winner.

10. Event number six is the frisbee discus. Like javelin, except now you're throwing a frisbee. And to make it harder you also have to release the frisbee from the back (little-finger side) of your hand as you throw it. (Spinning wind-up optional!) Mark the landing spot with tape. The longest throw after three rounds wins. Note the winner.

11. The final event, number seven, is the mini-marathon or distance race. Use Google Maps to create a long-distance course, with a starting point and end point at least two miles apart. Between your school and your house, perhaps. Or maybe just four times around the village. Make sure the route is safe, and that you can stay on grass or pavement (and off the roads) throughout. Once the course is set, everybody sets off together at the starting line, and races to the agreed finish line. To make it interesting, the winner of the mini-marathon gets two 'wins', rather than just one.

12. Now total up the wins on the notepad and declare the victor, based on who won the most. Stage the awards ceremony, complete with medals, and jog a victory lap around the house wearing your medals. Start planning your next heptathlon event right away. Same time next week?

GOING THE DISTANCE

Distance Running

Why can some people run marathons, but others start wheezing after a mile?
Because distance running not only requires strength, it also requires fitness and endurance. Some people are born 'fitter' than others, as fitness partly depends on how big your lungs and heart are, and how efficiently they work. But endurance is also a skill – you get better at it with practice.

So what's the difference between being fit and being healthy?
The two are related, but not quite the same.

Being healthy	=	the absence of disease
Being fit	=	being healthy and able to perform physical tasks

Can you be healthy without being fit?

Well, you can be reasonably healthy without necessarily being very fit. But keeping fit, along with healthy eating, is very important for staying healthy, especially as you get older. And fitness is extremely important to athletes. In short, you can't play many sports well without being fit.

The good news is that no matter how fit (or unfit) you are right now, with the right kind of training, you can get much fitter with practice, as fitness (like balance, timing and most other sporting qualities) is a skill.

Fitness is a skill? I've heard of 'getting fit' and 'keeping fit'. Are you telling me you can get 'extra fit' too?

Yep, that's exactly what I'm telling you. Not everyone can become as fit as an Olympic cyclist or swimmer. If you're born with a heart or lung problem, there may be some limits to how fit you can get. On the flipside, some athletes are simply born with amazingly efficient hearts, lungs and muscles.

But most healthy people can easily double (or even triple) their fitness and endurance levels with the right kind of training.

Eating Yourself Healthy

Nutrition, or healthy eating, is an essential part of training for most top-level athletes. Swimmers and distance runners, in particular, use up a lot of energy in their daily training, so they have to eat thousands of calories per day just to keep their muscles fuelled. But if you want to reach peak fitness, you can't just scarf down platefuls of burgers, chips and ice cream. For this reason, most athletes eat a carefully balanced diet, with plenty of **protein** to build and repair muscle, vegetables for **essential vitamins** and **fibre**, and **complex carbohydrates** to build slow-release energy stores.

Born to Run

Ultramarathon runner **Dean Karnazes** can run 350 miles (480km) without stopping, and once ran fifty marathons in fifty days.

It seems that Mr Karnazes was born a little special. Scientific tests have revealed that he has incredible **muscular endurance**, meaning that his muscles can work for an extraordinarily long time before getting tired. Because of this, his heart doesn't have to work so hard to resupply his muscles with oxygen, and it's never in any danger of failing or exploding.

> *'Run when you can, walk if you have to, crawl if you must; just never give up.'*
>
> Dean Karnazes, ultramarathon runner

What have hearts and lungs got to do with being fit?

How well your heart and lungs work has everything to do with being fit. Fitness and endurance are all about how well – and how quickly – you can get oxygen to your muscles. And in the human body that's the job of the heart, the lungs and the rest of the **cardiovascular system**.

Get It Sorted –
The Cardiovascular System

Your **cardiovascular system** (or **CV system**, for short) is one of your organ systems and includes your heart, lungs, arteries, veins and other blood vessels.

Its main job is to **deliver oxygen** – dissolved into the bloodstream from the **lungs** – to hungry muscles, tissues and organs all over your body.

The bloodstream also carries **nutrients**. This is important, as muscles and other tissues use these nutrients to create **energy stores**.

Without a constant supply of oxygen and energy, your muscles stop working pretty quickly. Oh, and you'd die.

Your cardiovascular system also stops toxic wastes from building up in your tissues, by delivering them to the lungs and kidneys for removal. These toxic nasties include **carbon dioxide** (the stuff you breathe out with every breath) and **lactic acid**, which we'll be talking about a bit more about later on.

So what does the, um, car...dio...va...scular system have to do with being fit?

See page 12 in chapter one for more about organ systems.

Being **fit** (biologically speaking) means having a **well-developed cardiovascular system** which is very good at supplying nutrients and oxygen to the muscles.

During hard exercise, the muscles use up the body's energy and oxygen stores very quickly.

Fit people have no trouble replacing these stores, because their CV systems are good at getting oxygen (especially) from the lungs to the muscles. So their muscles keep working for longer, and they can keep running, rowing or swimming for a long time.

Unfit people simply can't replace the used-up oxygen and energy quickly enough. Their hearts, lungs and blood vessels can't take in enough oxygen, can't get enough oxygen into the blood and can't shift the blood around the body quickly enough to supply the hungry muscles. Starved of energy and oxygen, the muscles begin to shut down, and **fatigue** sets in.

This is why unfit people pant for breath, then collapse in a heap, while fit people around them run on. They're trying to get more oxygen into their bodies, but they can't, so their leg muscles give out. Or, more often, their brains tell them to lie down before they collapse.

So why doesn't this happen when you're sprinting? I mean, more or less everyone can run a short distance without collapsing, right?

That's because it takes time for the oxygen and energy to run out. Most of your muscles have their own little energy stores, which are built up while you're resting. They're just sitting there waiting to be used. Similarly (unless you've been holding your breath for the last ten minutes) you start a sprint with oxygen already in your bloodstream.

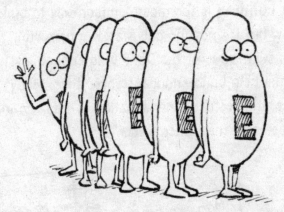

When you start sprinting, your leg muscles pump away furiously, using up energy and oxygen as they do so. But, for most people, unless you continue sprinting for more than thirty seconds, you've still got plenty of energy and oxygen stores left by the time you stop running. But run a bit further, say 400m rather than 100m, and the difference between fit and unfit people becomes very clear.

So the further you run the fitter you need to be?

Exactly. That's why fitness is extremely important for marathon runners, swimmers and other endurance athletes.

So what's the best way to get fit, if you're not already?

In general, how you train for fitness depends on which sport you're interested in doing.

Distance running is the most common way to build endurance, but it's not the only way. Runners run, swimmers swim, rowers row. Done long enough, even **walking** will help build endurance over time. Many endurance athletes use a combination of these to increase their fitness and endurance levels.

Monday

Morning: run
Afternoon: swim

Tuesday

Morning: run
Afternoon: row

Wednesday

Morning: run
Afternoon: swim

Thursday

Morning: run
Afternoon: row

Friday

Morning: run
Afternoon: swim

Saturday

Don't forget
to stretch!

Cardio Fitness

Done correctly, cardio training makes the cardiovascular system more efficient at **pumping blood** and **delivering oxygen** to the skeletal muscles.

Cardio training goals

1. Increase your body's maximum rate of **oxygen uptake**.

2. Increase the amount of work your muscles can do before tiredness (or **fatigue**) begins to set in.

When you're at rest (i.e. not doing much of anything), your muscles don't need much oxygen or bloodflow. So only 15-20% of your blood goes to the muscles. The rest goes to your brain, digestive organs and other bits of the body.

During hard exercise your muscles start burning through stored energy and oxygen very quickly. So the amount of blood flowing to your muscles has to increase to 80-85%, just to keep your muscles supplied with oxygen.

So how does it get there? Well, first, the **blood vessels** (**arteries**, **veins**, **arterioles** and **venules**) that feed and drain your working muscles open up. Meanwhile, the vessels that feed the brain and digestive system close up a bit. This redirects blood flow towards the muscles. It's a bit like damming a river to redirect water into a new reservoir.

To get this redirected blood and oxygen to the muscles in time, the heart has to pump harder and faster. So the fitter you are, the more efficiently your heart works.

What if you're not an endurance athlete? How fit do you need to be, and how much should you run or swim?

For young people under the age of eighteen just looking to stay fit and healthy, most doctors and sports scientists say that an hour of moderate exercise every day should be enough.

But if you want to do a bit more no one's going to stop you!

Smoking – the Fitness Killer

For decades now, we've known that smoking cigarettes leads to damage and diseases of the lungs.

Smoking decreases the amount of oxygen you can hold in your bloodstream, and how much of it can be passed rapidly to your needy muscles. At the very least, smoking will decrease your endurance levels by 10% or more. At worst, it could cause blood clots that lead to lung disease, heart disease or strokes.

So it should be obvious that if you want to get (or stay) fit then smoking is a pretty stupid idea.

Give it a go!

Exercise: fitness test
Type: cardiovascular
Goal: measuring your personal fitness level

1. Grab a stopwatch, or watch with a second hand.

2. Press two fingers into one side (not both!) of your neck, just below your jawline. Don't press too hard – just go deep enough to feel your pulse beating away in the arteries of your neck.

3. Count how many times your pulse beats in the next thirty seconds. To do this, count the **beats**, but watch the **clock**.

4. Now multiply this by two to find your resting pulse rate. (So if you counted 35 beats, multiply by two to get a resting pulse rate of 70.)

5. Immediately drop the watch and exercise for the next two minutes straight. You can run on the spot (lifting your knees as high as possible), do press-ups, do jump-squats (see previous chapter) – any one of these will do. Just don't stop. Keep going, as fast as you can, for two minutes.

average adult:
resting pulse
rate 60-
100bpm

child:
resting pulse
rate 70-
120bpm

**elite
endurance
athlete:**
resting pulse
rate 40bpm or
less

6. Now immediately repeat steps 1–4. This will give
you a number for your pulse rate during exercise.

The fitter you are, the longer it will take for your pulse
rate to rise to its maximum level. The maximum, in **bpm**,
is usually **220 minus your age**. So if you're ten years
old, it'll be around 210bpm, but if you're forty years old,
it'll be around 180bpm.

Swimming

Why don't swimming champions swim like sharks?

Because human swimmers – even Olympic champions – aren't built like fish, so trying to swim like a shark wouldn't make them go any faster. Instead, champion swimmers focus on being like sharks: sleek, streamlined and efficient in the water.

Wait . . . so they're not built like sharks, and can't swim like sharks . . . but they still try to be like sharks?

Exactly.

I'm confused.

OK, look at it this way: what makes sharks such speedy swimmers?

Err, their long tails?

That's part of it, yes. Fast-swimming sharks like the **mako shark** can hit very high speeds underwater by whipping their **tails** and **caudal fins** (tail fins) from side to side, quickly and powerfully. But not only do human swimmers not have tail fins, they also lack the muscles to make these powerful movements.

Caudal fin

Tail

Hang on, swimmers do have muscles. Pretty big ones too, if they're Olympic athletes.

Right. But their most powerful muscles don't run down the sides of their bodies, as they do in a shark.

Because we evolved to walk and run, rather than swim, our strongest muscles lie in front of and behind our spines, and in front of and behind our legs.

Hence, our bodies are good at bending forward and backwards (or curling and straightening), but they're pretty rubbish at wiggling from side to side, like a shark.

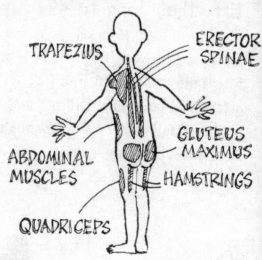

TRAPEZIUS

ERECTOR SPINAE

ABDOMINAL MUSCLES

GLUTEUS MAXIMUS

HAMSTRINGS

QUADRICEPS

Aha! But don't dolphins swim by wiggling their bodies up and down too? Couldn't we learn to move like them?

huge flat tail

Well, in some ways, champion swimmers (especially those who do the butterfly stroke) do just this – waving their bodies up and down to gain more power and speed in the water. But human swimmers still lack the huge, flat tail that transfers a dolphin's vertical wiggles into a powerful swimming stroke. So, for the most part, a swimmer's power comes from his or her arms. Leg kicks add speed, certainly. But without wearing fins on our feet (as scuba divers do, but swimmers do not) kicking alone wouldn't get you anywhere fast.

So how do champion swimmers make themselves faster than everyone else?

They train hard to increase their cardiovascular fitness, and also to perfect their swimming form (or shape) and the efficiency of their movements in the water.

How does changing their shape make a difference?

Sharks and swimmers are slowed down by drag. As they try to power through the water, friction from the water around them drags on their bodies and slows them down.

Sharks have managed to get round this by evolving a streamlined body shape. They're shaped like swimming missiles. Their bodies are long, thin tubes with a cone-shaped nose at the front (which parts the water before the shark as

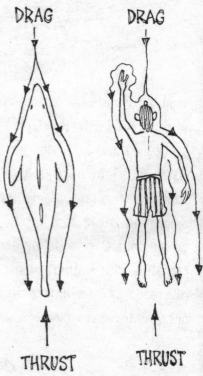

it goes) and short, flat fins along the side and top, which allow the smooth movement of water around them.

Now compare this with a human swimmer. We have rounded heads and flat faces, which drag in the water every time we raise them to breathe. We have flailing arms and legs, which drag in the water as we try to use them to push through it. We can swim, but we're not built to do it the way a shark is.

Shark Suits

From the 1990s onwards, some champion swimmers, including Olympic gold medallists Michael Phelps and Ian 'Thorpedo' Thorpe, began wearing full-length bodysuits to reduce the effect of drag in the water. These suits feature tiny plastic ridges (or 'riblets'), which mimic the interlocking scales

of a shark skin. The riblets help to break up pockets of turbulent (or churning) water that cause extra drag, and aid the flow of water around the swimmer. Physicists say these suits make little or no difference to the total drag experienced by a swimmer, anyway. But officials were worried enough by the full-length 'fast suits' that they banned them in Olympic competitions from 2010 onwards. Now male competitors' suits cannot extend above the waist or below the knee, while female competitors' suits can go from the shoulders to the knees.

So what's the answer?

The answer is to try to make the shape of your swimming stroke as streamlined and shark-like as possible. And that's exactly what champion swimmers do. They practise their strokes in the pool, trying to make themselves glide through the water with less drag. This means making sure that fingers and toes stay together and hands pierce the water fingertip first. Any body parts, like elbows and knees, that stick out while they swim will slow them down, making their movements less powerful and efficient.

Swimmers will practise for hours – often wearing snorkels, so that they don't have to worry about lifting their heads to breathe – to create the perfect, shark-like, gliding stroke.

I've got a snorkel. But they won't let me wear it at the pool.

Next time, just tell them you're in training for the Olympics, and you're working on your swimming stroke. Maybe they'll let you.

Good idea!

'My goal is one Olympic gold medal. Not many people in this world can say, "I'm an Olympic gold medallist."'

Michael Phelps, *champion swimmer and winner of eighteen Olympic gold medals*

Rowing, Canoeing and Kayaking

Are rowing, canoeing and kayaking all the same thing?

Nope – not at all. They all involve racing a long boat through the water. But rowers, canoeists and kayakers propel their boats in quite different ways. Rowers sit facing backwards, while canoeists and kayakers sit facing forward. Rowers grip boat-mounted oars, while canoeists and kayakers wield single or double-ended paddles. And while rowers use almost every muscle in their bodies to pull their boats through the water, for the most part, canoeists and kayakers use their upper bodies alone.

ROWER   CANOEIST   KAYAKER

Rowers sit backwards? Wouldn't that make their boats go backwards too?

Eh?

Well, that depends on how you look at it. A rowing boat travels in the opposite direction to the way the pilot (rower, or crew of rowers) is facing, whereas canoes and kayaks travel in the same direction the pilot is facing. Either way, the pilot is **pushing water backwards** to make the boat travel **forward**.

How does that work?

Simple – as the famous physicist, mathematician and all-round genius **Isaac Newton** first said, in the world of movement and physics,

'**Every action has an equal and opposite reaction**.'

In rowing and canoeing, it's easy to see this idea in action.

To make the boat go forward, the rower or canoeist places a flattened blade (on the end of a long pole or handle) into the water, and uses it to push water backwards. The equal and opposite reaction to this is simple: the boat (complete with rower or canoeist) moves forward.

The main difference between rowing, canoeing and kayaking is how that water is pushed backwards. Canoeists and kayakers sit facing the direction of travel, and paddle with alternating backward pushes to the left and right side of the boat. They push the water behind themselves, and the boat travels forward. Rowers, on the other hand, sit backwards in the boat, pulling on **bevelling oars** that shift the water (as they see it) in front of themselves, or towards their feet.

It's Not Oar the Same

A **rowing oar** is basically a long pole with a flattened blade at one end. In a rowing boat, the oars thread through special pivoting rings attached to the sides of the boat, called **oarlocks** or **rowlocks**.

A rower may sit holding the handles of **two oars** (one in each hand). This kind of two-oar rowing is called **sculling**.

Alternatively, a rower may hold a single oar – gripping the handle with both hands – which extends out to one side of the boat only. This is simply called **rowing**.

Single-oar rowers always work in **pairs, fours** or **eights**. Provided that there's an even number of rowers – and an equal number of left and right oars in the water – their left-and-right-side, backward-pushing forces will be balanced, and the equal and opposite reaction will move the bow straight ahead.

If a rower rowed only on the left, the bow of the boat would always veer right and the boat would go round in circles.

Canoeists use a single, stubby paddle. The paddle has a shorter shaft (usually 1–1.5m) with a T-shaped horizontal handle at the top. The canoeist grips the handle with one hand and the shaft with the other, holding the paddle vertically above the water, to one side of the body (and the boat). He or she then paddles by dipping the blade down into the water and scooping the water backwards in a vertical churning motion.

To prevent them going round in circles, canoeists either work in pairs (like rowers) or paddle first on the left side, then the right, using **alternating strokes**. This nudges the bow from side to side a little, but, provided they keep the power and number of strokes on each side the same, the boat will travel (more or less) straight.

A **kayak paddle** is a long pole with a flat blade at both ends. Kayakers hold these double-ended paddles in two hands, with one clenched fist on either side of the chest.

From there, the kayaker dips first the left end, then the right end of the paddle into the water, and uses a **rolling, crawling motion** to make alternating strokes to the left and right sides of the kayak. Again, the bow noses to the left and right a little with each push, but if the kayaker keeps their strokes even, the kayak will move happily forward.

Which one is the hardest work?

Well, the answer to that one will depend on whether you ask a rower, a canoeist or a kayaker! But one thing's for certain: rowing uses (and requires) more muscles than either canoeing or kayaking. For this reason, many would say rowing is the toughest of the three.

Why does rowing use more muscles?

In short, because a full rowing stroke involves both the upper and lower body.

For the most part, canoeists and kayakers sit fairly still in their boats, using powerful twisting motions of the arms, shoulders and torso to drive their paddles through the water.

Rowing is completely different. In a competitive rowing boat, each rower braces their feet against a footplate on the floor of the boat, and sits on a sliding seat, which rolls back and forth as the rowers bend and straighten their knees. By pushing with the feet and shifting their bodies backwards with each pull of the oars, a rower connects the powerful muscles of the legs to those of the torso and arms, and puts his or her whole bodyweight behind each pull.

'The pain of rowing is the scream of lungs, legs, back and muscles. That's just one stroke. Multiply that by 240 strokes in a 2,000m race.'
Steve Redgrave (right), legendary British rower and winner of gold medals at five consecutive Olympic Games between 1984 and 2000

Using the whole body like this is much harder work, but it multiplies both the force of each backward rowing stroke and the equal and opposite force that drives the boat forward. For this reason, rowing boats ultimately accelerate and travel much faster than canoes or kayaks. In addition, rowing boats can have crews of up to eight rowers working together, which increases the speed even further.

So do two rowers go twice as fast as one, and eight rowers twice as fast as four?

That would seem to make sense, wouldn't it? But, in fact, this doesn't quite happen. This is because of two things. First, every crew member you add also adds weight to the boat. Now because heavier things take more force to accelerate (Isaac Newton told us that too), this makes it harder to get the boat up to top speed.

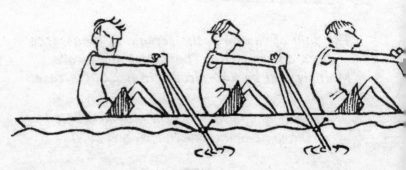

Second, unless the entire crew's oar blades enter and leave the water at exactly the same time, then one rower's oar will be trying to push the boat forward while another drags in the water, slowing the whole boat down.

The Coxswain

Rowing teams need to **match** or **synchronize** the movements of their oar blades as much as possible to minimize the drag caused by sloppy, poorly timed strokes. To help with this, teams of four or more rowers may also include an extra crew member - the **coxswain**.

The coxswain (or **cox**, for short) sits in the back (or stern) of the boat, facing the rest of the crew, and shouts instructions to help them keep their oar strokes in time. When the cox wants the crew to speed up, he or she makes sure they all speed up together. He or she also has to be very light, so as not to weigh down the boat too much!

Cross-country Skiing

How hard would it be to ski UP a mountain?

Hard. VERY hard. But not impossible. In fact, cross-country skiers ski uphill all the time. It just takes a bit of knowledge, a lot of practice and almost superhuman levels of endurance.

Really? It'd be that hard? Even if you got a good run-up first?

Yep.

Why?

Think about it. What are skis for? What do they do?

Err . . . you wear them on your feet when you want to travel over snow. They let you zip down snowy slopes really fast.

Right. Long, flat skis increase the **surface area** of your feet. This helps to spread your body weight over a wider area, which stops you from sinking into soft snow. They also have a smooth lower surface that decreases friction and slips easily over the snow.

This is wonderful, of course, when you want to travel downhill. **Gravity** pulls you downward, and without much friction sticking your skis to the slope, all you have to do is stay upright and steer.

Right. Skiing down hills is simple enough. But when you try to ski uphill . . .

. . . then gravity starts to work against you, trying to pull you back down the slope. And the lack of friction you so enjoyed on the way down turns out to be a nightmare on the way up. Without much friction to hold your skis on the slope, they slip several centimetres backwards for every centimetre you ski forward.

So how do cross-country skiers do it?

They increase the friction in each step by turning the tips of the skis outward and digging the edges of their skis into the snow. Then they **shuffle** (or if it's not too steep, **skate**) up the slope by pushing off from the edge of one ski at a time.

When they reach the top of a hill, they can then happily ski down the other side just like a normal skier would – skis straight and parallel, body and arms tucked in to cut down on air resistance and drag. On flat or level plains, they use one of two methods. They can freestyle it, usually by pushing back and to one side with the inner edges of their skis and skate their way forwards. Others keep their skis parallel and shuffle first one ski, then the other. This is called classic cross-country skiing.

Which method they use may depend on the type of event (in some races, you're only allowed to use the classical method) or the depth of snow (freestyle works well on firm snow, but not too well on very soft snow).

How far can they go like this? You know, like in a proper race?

In the Winter Olympics, cross-country skiers race up to thirty miles (50km) downhill, uphill and across level ground. So, regardless of which techniques the players use, cross-country skiing is still one of the most gruelling sports in the world.

Thirty miles? That's like a ski-marathon!

Whoa!

It's longer than a marathon. And, just like marathon runners, cross-country skiers have to train for years to build up their endurance, just to avoid collapsing in a heap halfway through the race.

In fact, cross-country skiers have the highest measured levels of **cardiovascular fitness** and **muscular endurance** of any type of athlete.

Hang on, aren't endurance and fitness the same thing?

They're related, but not the same. We've already seen how cardio training improves endurance, by improving the ability of your heart and lungs to supply your muscles with oxygen. But to be an elite runner, swimmer or cross-country skier, cardiovascular fitness alone is not enough. You also need **muscular endurance**. Over many years, endurance training can change the structure of athletes' muscles so that they can work harder for longer, giving them **muscular endurance**.

But how do the muscles change? Do they get bigger?

Not usually, no. In fact, with endurance training, the muscles often become smaller. Endurance is less about the size of the muscle, and more about the types of fibres within.

Slow-twitch (type I) muscle fibres use their stored energy slowly and take much longer to tire out than fast-twitch muscles, so they keep you moving for longer.

For this reason, endurance events rely more upon slow-firing (slow-twitch) muscle fibres, and training for endurance involves building slow-twitch muscle fibres and energy stores in the muscles.

Feel the Burn

During exercise, your muscles not only burn up lots of oxygen, they also create more **toxic waste products** – mostly in the form of **carbon dioxide** and something called **lactic acid** (or lactate). Your muscles are constantly creating these products as they work – they're like the dirty ash and soot left behind as you burn a pile of logs on a campfire. It's the build-up of lactic acid that makes your muscles hurt when you exercise hard.

In endurance races like marathons and ski-marathons, the build-up of carbon dioxide and lactic acid in the blood reaches a point sports scientists call the **lactate threshold**. After this point, athletes **'feel the burn'** and the muscles start to fatigue.

So endurance training turns your fast-twitch muscles into slow-twitch ones?

We first met type I (slow-twitch) and type II (fast-twitch) muscle fibres on page 22.

Actually, you can't turn type II muscle fibres into type I fibres. But with proper training, you can increase the number of new type I fibres in your muscles, making them better suited to distance events.

What's more, the same training will increase the number of **small blood vessels** (or **capillaries**) that supply each muscle with oxygen, and increase the number and size of **mitochondria** (the tiny, energy-converting powerhouses within cells) within each individual muscle cell.

In a sense, endurance training makes you **superhuman**. It turns you into a more efficient machine, allowing you to use less energy to do the same amount of work.

Cool. But, if it's all the same to you, I think I'll stick to skiing downhill. Seems like far less effort. And a lot more fun . . .

HE SHOOTS...
HE SCORES!

Archery and Shooting

If you're a 'crack shot' with a rifle or a bow and arrow, is that because your eyes are sharper than other people's?

Not necessarily. Although top shooters and archers do tend to have keen eyesight, becoming a 'crack shot' is more about training your brain and nervous system than it is about having sharp eyes. And, in fact, the same thing applies to shooting basketballs, footballs and hockey pucks too.

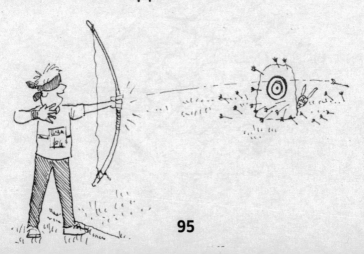

Eh? What's your brain got to do with shooting arrows and basketballs?

A lot, actually. What do you think you're shooting with?

Well, your hands . . . and your eyes. You look with your eyes, and shoot with your hands. Right?

Well, it's true that your eyes take in the image of the target. And your hands aim – and eventually release – the shot. But neither is actually doing the looking or shooting. The eyes just relay information to the brain, via the **nervous system**. Your brain then 'sees' the target. This done, the brain aims the shot by sending signals to the muscles in your hands, again, via the **nervous system**.

This is often known as hand-eye coordination.

The Body's Internet

Your nervous system includes your brain, spinal cord and nerves. Together, these form a high-speed communication system that controls and connects every organ and tissue. It's like the body's very own internet.

Internet

Used to send and receive messages, store and save memories (in the form of digital documents, pictures and video clips), work, chat, learn, play games and much, much more.

Nervous system

Sends and receives messages between muscles and organs via the **nerves**, stores and saves memories in the **brain**, and coordinates thought, speech, learning and movement.

But unlike the internet, which has no single controller, for most purposes, the brain is the 'big boss' of the nervous system.

The list of things for which you can use your brain and nervous system is almost limitless. But for the purposes of sport and exercise, it has three basic functions: **moving**, **sensing** and **interpreting**.

Even without knowing about these things in detail, we can see right away how you can use your nervous system to shoot, and learn to shoot better.

How's that?

It's quite simple, really. Learning to shoot means sensing (or looking at) a target, then moving your hands into the correct position (aiming) and taking the shot. Then you look again to see where your shot ended up, or by how much you missed the target. Armed with this new image, your brain can then interpret (or make sense of) that information, and figure out which way to adjust your aiming movements before shooting again.

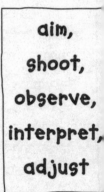

aim,
shoot,
observe,
interpret,
adjust

In **archery competitions** archers shoot batches of three arrows, one after the other. Even if the first arrow goes off-target they can use the visual information from the first shot to adjust their aim and get closer to the bullseye with the next two.

Shooting, then, is about training yourself to miss by less with every shot, using these three processes of sensing, moving and interpreting. The more you practise, the smaller the distance you miss by, and the smaller the adjustment you have to make to your aiming movements.

It's a Bullseye!

The term 'bullseye' dates back to the seventeenth century, when it was used to describe any small, circular object – including coins, sweets and small, round windows set into the lower decks of ships. By 1830, it had been adopted by archers and darts players to describe the centre of the target. Thankfully, it seems that no real bulls were harmed in the making of this phrase . . .

Of course, if you want to take up this sport, you have to make sure you do it safely, as guns – even air pistols – can be very dangerous. So the best way to do it is to join a shooting club, where experienced instructors can show you how to shoot targets safely.

But if you want to have a go at improving your aim you don't even need an air pistol to do it. Try the exercise opposite, and you'll be a 'crack shot' in no time!

Give it a go!

Exercise:	aim small, miss small
Type:	skill
Goal:	improving your aim

1. Draw a circular, archery-style target on a wall in chalk, or draw one on a large piece of cardboard and tape it to the wall.

2. Grab a tennis ball, walk at least five metres away from the wall and chalk a line on the ground. This is your shooting line, and you're not allowed to put a foot beyond it.

3. Now take aim and throw, trying to hit the very centre of the target. Watch where it hits. (This will be easier if you chalked the target, as this bit will smudge.)

4. If the ball went high, aim a little lower than the centre next time. If it went to the left, aim a little to the right. But don't overdo it – just aim a few centimetres away from the centre, in the opposite direction to where your last shot hit.

5. Now throw again, look again and adjust your aim just a little bit.

6. Repeat at least fifty times. This done, take a break, then repeat every day for a week! I guarantee you'll be a much better shot by the following week.

You can also try this with a football, or with a tennis racquet and ball. It all depends which sport (and what kind of shot) you're interested in improving.

Now get some friends together and see how they fare against you!

Basketball

How do basketball players 'hang' in the air when they do a jumping slam dunk?

They don't. No matter how high they leap, basketball players cannot hover or fly. Like everybody else, they start falling back down immediately after they jump up. It only looks like they 'hang' in the air because they're moving forward as well as upward.

But when you see them on TV they seem to stay in the air for ages. If I jump up, I plop back to the ground again right away.

Well, most professional basketball players (at least the ones who play in attacking positions) can jump pretty high. So they probably get a bit more time in the air than you on the average jump. But we're only talking about fractions of a second. No matter how high you jump, you

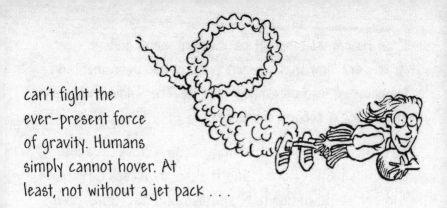

can't fight the
ever-present force
of gravity. Humans
simply cannot hover. At
least, not without a jet pack . . .

. . . or rocket-powered trainers.

Right. If they even existed. Which they don't.

That would be awesome, though.

Yes. It would.

So why does it look like the players are hovering when they're not?

It's a trick of the eye (or, more accurately, the brain) which makes it hard to judge how long they stay in the air.

I don't get it.

Look at it this way: if a player jumps straight up, all his **velocity** (a combination of speed and direction) is **vertical**. He accelerates upward at the start of the jump, but since gravity is constantly pulling him downward, his jump velocity starts slowing immediately, and he reaches a peak of maybe just over a metre off the ground.

Then he comes straight back down again, and we clearly see how that upward velocity has been lost, and transferred into downward velocity. The whole thing takes just under a second to happen.

We're used to seeing this kind of thing. Toss an apple or tennis ball in the air and it slows, reverses direction and comes down again. What goes up must come down. Simple.

OK . . .

But when a basketball player takes a running leap towards the net for a slam dunk, he doesn't travel up and down in a straight line. He has **horizontal velocity** (or forward motion) as well as **vertical velocity** (or upward motion).

Because of this, his path through the air is not a straight line, but an arc. When a player is moving forward as well as upward like this, it's harder for our eyes and brains to separate the horizontal and vertical speeds, and harder to recognize how long it takes for the player to reach the top of his jump.

In reality, gravity affects the vertical part of this jump in exactly the same way as it did when the player jumped straight up. He goes up and comes down in less than a

second, just as before. But, since the player spends up to half of that second in the top part of the arc, it appears as if he spends at least a quarter of a second hovering in the air, in what basketball fans call 'hang time'.

Slow the whole thing down in an **action replay**, and you'll see that the player starts falling as soon as he's finished accelerating upward. So, in reality, there is no 'hang'.

Why do they jump up like that to shoot, anyway? Seems like a lot of effort. Why not just toss it into the basket with their feet on the ground?

Well, if you can pull it off, jumping at the basket and simply placing the ball through the hoop is a lot easier than trying to toss the ball into the hoop with a well-aimed, arcing throw. In fact, even when they shoot from a distance, basketball players will often still jump up straight before shooting, as it allows the ball to approach the hoop at a higher angle. This reduces the chances of the ball bouncing off the rim of the hoop, and increases the chances that it'll drop through instead.

No Dunks, Please

Slam dunking, or jumping at a basketball hoop and slamming the ball down through it, first appeared in the 1940s, with 7-foot-tall American Olympic gold medallist Bob Kurland. It was banned in US games between 1967 and 1976, but later allowed under new rules. The phrase 'slam dunk' has now become a popular phrase, meaning 'can't miss' or 'guaranteed'.

Tennis

Just how fast does a tennis serve go?

As of July 2015, the fastest tennis serve ever recorded clocked in at an incredible 163.7mph (263.4km/h). At Wimbledon, top tennis players frequently hit serves that rocket past the net at 130mph (210km/h) or more.

It's a wonder that any of them are hit back at all! How can you ever learn to hit a shot like that? I mean, it's coming so fast, it seems like you wouldn't have time to think.

Actually, you don't. Top players practise until their returns become almost automatic. When a top tennis player dives at a smash to prevent it hitting the floor, he or she isn't really thinking at all.

But I thought you said earlier that your brain and nerves controlled all your movements and responses.

They do. But that doesn't mean the brain has to think to do it. Here's how it all fits together . . .

The bit of the brain that controls muscle movement is called the **motor cortex**. This region sits on the top edge of the brain, in a broad stripe that runs around the middle of the brain like a girl's hairband. Each part of the motor cortex controls muscles in a specific part of the body – there are regions that relate to the hand muscles, foot muscles, facial muscles, and everything in between.

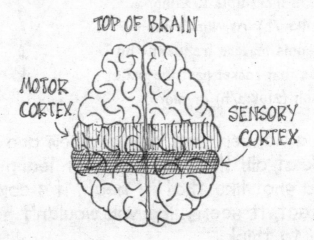

TOP OF BRAIN

MOTOR CORTEX

SENSORY CORTEX

OK. That makes sense, I s'pose.

This is where your **nerves** come in. Signals travel from the motor cortex to the muscles through **motor nerves** or **motor neurons**. One end of each motor neuron lies in the brain, while the other attaches to a group of **muscle fibres** within a muscle.

The longest motor neurons – the ones that run from the brain to the muscles in the toes – can measure over 2m long!

One motor neuron may attach to as few as five or as many as 1,000 muscle fibres. Together, a single neuron and its fibres form one **motor unit**. Firing a signal through it will make every muscle fibre in the motor unit contract at once.

By coordinating the firing of different motor units, the brain controls every kind of movement your body can make. One set of signals might bend a single index finger. Another will wrap all five fingers round the grip of a tennis racquet. Yet **another** will angle and swing an arm to deliver a powerful cross-court tennis serve that screams past your opponent at over 150mph.

Tactics vs Raw Power

In all racquet sports the players aim to hit the ball, or shuttle if they are playing badminton, into areas from which the opponent will find it difficult or impossible to hit back.

Winning tactics include (a) driving your opponent to the back of his court, then playing a quick, near-net **'drop shot'** that he has no hope of reaching, and (b) forcing your opponent to lift the ball or shuttle with an awkward return, so that you can leap into the air and **smash** it mercilessly to the ground in his (or her) court area.

So that's how you hit a 150mph serve. But that doesn't explain how you can hit one back.

Right. Returning a serve relies heavily on the second major function of your nervous system – **sensing**.

The bit of the brain that senses body movement is called the **sensory** (or if you're really posh, **somatosensory**) cortex. Again, it sits on the top edge of the brain, forming a second hairband that lies just behind that of the motor cortex.

Signals travel to the sensory cortex from the muscles, tendons, fascia, skin and other organs and tissues throughout the body, via **sensory neurons**. There's at least one sensory neuron within every muscle and tendon in your body, and some muscles contain hundreds of sensory neurons.

Together, these sensory neurons send millions of sensory signals to the brain every second, giving it **non-stop feedback**. This tells the brain where each muscle, bone and limb is in space, what the angles are between them, and how tense or relaxed each muscle and tendon is.

PING! PING! PING PING! PING! PING!

But how does knowing where your limbs are help you return a super-fast tennis serve?

Because the sensory part of the nervous system also receives signals from the eyes, ears and other sensory organs. By combining these signals, your nervous system allows you to observe what's going on and orient yourself towards it. So you return the serve on seeing it ('there's a tennis ball flying at me'), then proceed to take stock of where you are ('I'm facing the ball, feet apart, racquet down'). Next, you have to decide what you're going to do ('turn sideways, raise the racquet, prepare to hit the ball'), and do it ('turn, lift racquet, hit ball!').

But don't the deciding and doing parts mean that you have to think?

Not necessarily. Train hard enough, and your nervous system will decide and act for you. This brings us to the third major job of the nervous system in the body: **interpreting**.

In addition to **moving** and **sensing** things, your nervous system also **interprets** – or makes sense of – the information relayed by the sensory neurons, and uses this information to build new motor skills and movements. This happens almost entirely within the brain, and uses many different regions of the brain – from the outer cortex to the deeper **forebrain**, **midbrain** and **hindbrain**.

By combining the information from motor signals and sensory signals, the brain can 'test out' new, complex muscle movements and learn – by trial and error – how best to accomplish them. This is how you learn precise, sport-related skills and movements, like returning a tennis serve, shooting a football, catching a basketball, or whacking a cricket ball right out of the grounds.

In the beginning, all complex movements like this are difficult, but, with repetition, they eventually become automatic, something your body knows how to do without thinking. We call this body-movement autopilot **muscle memory** (we first met this in chapter two, remember?). This is what allows a top tennis player to return a 150mph serve.

I could return a serve like that easily. If I wanted to.
No way!

Wanna bet?
Fine. How would you do it?

Easy. You just wait until the ball's gone past at 150mph.

OK . . .

Then you turn round, pick the ball up, walk over to the net, and hand it to the other player. Bingo – serve returned.

But that's cheating!

'Luck has nothing to do with it, because I have spent many, many hours, countless hours, on the court working for my one moment in time, not knowing when it would come.'

Serena Williams, world number-one women's tennis player, winner of 21 grand slam singles tournaments, and winner of four Olympic golds, one in women's singles and three in women's doubles

Football

How do you make a football bend in the air?

'Bending' a football during a corner or free kick is a tricky task indeed. It involves adding spin to the ball, which changes the way air moves around it, in-flight. This is easier said than done, and if you want to 'bend it like Beckham', you'll have to put a lot of practice in.

You spin the ball? Like with your fingers?

No, of course not. In football, you're not allowed to touch the ball with your hands. That is, unless you're the goalie.

If you live in the USA, then 'football' automatically means '**American football**'. If you live in the UK (or pretty much anywhere else in the world), it usually means 'soccer'. But there are other football games too, including **rugby**, **Gaelic football** and **Australian Rules football**.

Football (or **soccer** as most Americans call it) is a fast and relatively simple game. One goal gets you one point, and after playing for two forty-five minute halves, the team with the most points wins. You can control the ball with any part of the body except your arms and hands (in practice, mostly **feet**, **head** and **chest**).

It's this beautiful simplicity that has helped to make football the most popular, and most watched, sporting game in the world. Millions of people in the UK, Europe, South America and elsewhere play football, and follow football league games in their own countries. Football is played at the Olympics, and every four years, billions of people tune in to watch the **World Cup** tournament. In a way, football unifies the whole world.

So if football is so simple, does that mean it's easy to play?

Not necessarily. It requires **agility** – the ability to change your direction of movement quickly and suddenly. And football **strikers** and **centre-forwards**, of course, have to learn to **spin** and **bend** a ball through the air, sending it around defensive players and into a goal (or on to the head of a waiting teammate).

Hmmmm. I still don't quite get how that works.

What d'you mean?

I mean, why would spinning the ball affect how it moves through the air?

Why wouldn't it?

Well, I get that spin makes a ball bounce funny. That makes sense. It hits the ground with a spin, and comes off at a different angle.

OK . . .

. . . but if a spinning ball is just flying through the air, it's not actually touching anything, is it?

Ah, but it is. It's touching the air around it.

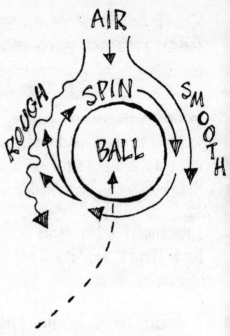

It is?

Of course. When a striker puts spin on a ball, by making contact with it a little to one side of the ball, it carves its way through the air as it spins. On one side of the ball, the air will be moving in the same direction that the ball is spinning. This makes the air flow over this side of the ball more smoothly, decreasing the pressure of the air against that side of the ball.

On the opposite side, the surface of the ball will be spinning, as it were, into the wind. This creates **drag** and **turbulence** (churning air), and increases the air pressure on that side of the ball.

Since there's now more pressure on one side of the ball than the other, the ball then drifts (or bends) to one side – towards the side with lower pressure. In effect, this means the path of the ball will bend away from the foot you struck it with. Hit the ball off-centre with the inside of your right foot, and it'll bend right to left. Hit it with inside of your left foot, it'll bend left to right.

Is that it? That sounds easy!

Well, it takes many, many hours of practice to learn to hit the ball just right for a bend. But if you're willing to put that much time into it, there's no reason why you couldn't learn to do it too. Who knows? In a few years' time, you could be curling in the winning shot at a World Cup final . . .

'I still look at myself and want to improve.'
David Beckham, football legend and former captain
of the England football team

Give it a go!

Exercise: bend it like Beckham
Type: skill
Goal: improve soccer skill

(These instructions are for right-footed players. If you're left-footed, reverse everything!)

1. To curve the ball from right to left, use the inside of your right foot, striking the bottom half of the right side of the ball.

2. To curve the ball from left to right, use the outside of your right foot, striking the bottom half of the left side of the ball.

3. In both cases, your follow-through will not be in the direction of the target goal or player. Instead, imagine you are cutting across the back of the ball rather than kicking through the centre of it.

4. Practise until brilliant. Earn spot on England team. Score a ridiculous number of goals from corners and free kicks. Reclaim glory by winning first World Cup for England since 1966.

Hockey

How do hockey players avoid hurting each other?

In field hockey, they wear pads on their shins and avoid swinging the stick too high. In ice hockey, they wear lots of body armour and slam into each other to their heart's content. Most of the time, they succeed in not getting too badly hurt . . .

Most of the time?

Err . . . yes. While players of all these sports try to play safely, some – ahem – try a bit harder than others. So you do get the occasional broken leg. Or rib. Or skull.

Yikes!

But I thought hockey was a safe game.

Well, for the most part, field hockey is safe. In **field hockey**, every player wields a **hockey stick**. But when they swing it they're aiming for the ball, not each other.

Field hockey dos and don'ts

Hockey players MAY use their sticks to:

Push – scoot the ball along the ground

Flick – scoop the ball into the air

Drive – swing at the ball like a golfer, for hard shots

Dribble – run, keeping the ball in front of them with deft taps to either side

Hockey players MAY NOT use their sticks to:

Hit the ball while it's in the air (or volley)

Raise their sticks above shoulder level to control a high ball

Hit each other with the sticks

But how do they avoid hitting each other? I mean, with all those players and sticks on the field, someone's going to get hit sometime. Even if it's only by accident.

That's true. In **team sports**, you rarely have the luxury of lining up the perfect throw or shot. With so many players moving around on the field at once, it's hard to predict, moment by moment, where everyone on the field will end up, where you'll have to shoot from, and how much time you'll have to take the shot. Shoot too soon or too late, and you could miss entirely. Or, worse yet, hurt somebody.

Because of this, team games require an extra-special sporting ability – **dexterity**. Dexterity is the ability to adapt your movements quickly to any given situation, or use your motor skills to solve problems. This is how hockey players get around each other on the field, and avoid hitting each other when they don't want to.

So other athletes don't need dexterity?

They do, yes. Just not as much. Let me explain . . .

Running in a straight line or throwing a javelin requires strength, skill and power. But if you were being chased by a pack of hungry wolves, or you had to throw that javelin at a sprinting, dodging rabbit, that would require dexterity.

WOOOOOOSH!

In team ball sports, a **high level of dexterity** is needed for **dodging**, **chasing**, **angling** and **adapting** to the movements of opponents and the fast, crazy chaotic movements of a flying, bouncing ball.

What's more, many ball sports are also played in **teams** competing head-to-head. This, too, requires dexterity, as every player on the team has to adapt to the movements of every other player on his own team, plus all those on the opposing team. That's a lot of thinking and moving to do on the fly!

So how do we do it?

In the body and brain, dexterity usually develops hand-in-hand with **balance** and **agility**. First, you learn to control your own movements, then you learn how to quickly change the direction of those movements and adapt them to those of your environment.

You can learn more about all these in the next chapter.

How on earth do hockey players dodge and weave like that on ice skates? I mean, wouldn't they just slip over if they tried to turn too quickly?

Well, ice skates slide around on top of the ice because they focus all your weight into a pair of thin, metal blades beneath your feet. This creates enormous pressure over a small surface area of the ice, causing it to melt into thin strips of water beneath each blade. Provided that you keep the skates level, you can glide forward or backwards on this thin layer of 'instant water' with very little **friction** to slow you down.

When they want to **turn** or **stop**, hockey players (and indeed all ice-skaters) dig the edges of their blades into the ice, creating ridges in the ice that push back against the skate – **increasing** friction and slowing or altering their movements.

126

Starting and stopping quickly can be tough, so falls and collisions do happen in ice hockey. But in general, ice-hockey players are very skilled skaters, and move much faster about the playing area than their counterparts in grass-based **field hockey**.

Is that pretty much all ice hockey is, then? Fast field-hockey-on-ice?

Actually, it's far more than that.

1. The **ice hockey rink** is surrounded by a wall of 1m wooden boards so the players can bounce the puck off the bordering walls, ricocheting it around their opponents.

This wooden wall is topped by a taller transparent one made of plexiglas, to protect the spectators from high-flying pucks.

2. The players can move past and behind the goal.

3. Skaters are allowed to control the puck with their feet (skates) or bodies.

4. Ice hockey is a **full-contact** game. Players are allowed to **body-check** (i.e. barge into) each other, slamming each other off their feet and even into the plexiglas walls around the rink.

Ouch!

The Penalty Box

Although it is supposed to be illegal to hit opponents with elbows, knees and parts of your stick, this can and does happen. Illegal tackles earn fouls and get the player temporarily sent off, leaving their team short of players on the ice. During this time, players have to skate off the ice and into a penalty box, staying there for two minutes (for a minor penalty) or five minutes (for a major one).

So while dangerous play gets players permanently sent off in field hockey and soccer, in ice hockey, it just earns you a temporary 'time-out'! As you might imagine, this makes the game quite a bit rougher. – hence the need for the extra padding and protection worn by the players.

'I wasn't naturally gifted in terms of size and speed; everything I did in hockey I worked for.'

Wayne Gretzky, *champion ice-hockey player and three-times gold-medal winner in the Canada Cup championships*

BALANCE, FLEXIBILITY AND CONTROL

Are gymnasts born super-bendy?

Some are, but most are not. Most gymnasts are born just like you and me, but use special exercises to lengthen their muscles, tendons and ligaments, and increase their flexibility over many years.

In fact no gymnast is double-jointed, because nobody is. People may appear 'double-jointed' if they have unusually flexible tendons and ligaments.

So they're not all double-jointed, then?

Most aren't, no. **Flexibility** isn't really about having extra bones or extra-stretchy muscles. It's the ability to move a body part or joint through a wide range of motion, without being hindered by the surrounding muscles, tendons and other tissues. What's more (and here's the good news if you want to be a top gymnast one day) flexibility is also a **trainable skill**.

130

So even if you're not born flexible, you can become flexible with the proper training.

Like yoga and stretching and stuff? Doesn't that hurt?

Not if you do it right, no.
When people stretch before
exercising – or try to
stretch their legs or spines
in a yoga class – they
can overdo it and cause
themselves pain and injury.
But this is usually because
they have the wrong idea
about what they're doing.

Flexibility training shouldn't be like putting yourself on a medieval torture rack! Because, if you're training properly, then you're not actually trying to stretch the muscles beyond their natural length.

You're not?

Of course not. Do that, and all you'll end up with is a **pulled** or **strained muscle**, or, worse yet, a **torn ligament** or **tendon**. All very nasty injuries.

So what are you trying to do when you stretch?

You're trying to get the brain to
reset the length of your muscles
and tendons, which allows them
to stretch further before tearing. This, in
turn, creates some **slack** in the joints, and
leaves the athlete **more flexible**.

To understand how this works, we need to know a bit
more about how muscles are **built**.

As we learned in chapter one, a muscle is like a big,
meaty bag made of lots and lots of individual **muscle
fibres**, all bundled together.

Sure. I remember that much.

Good. OK – now, in turn, each thin muscle fibre contains
several bundled muscle **fibrils** (or **myofibrils**), and
each muscle fibril contains a bundle of thread-like
myofilaments. **Myofilaments** lie side by side within
relaxed muscle fibrils, with their ends overlapping.

When they're supplied with energy – plus a signal from an
attached nerve – the ends of the myofilaments slide over
each other, increasing the overlap between them. This
shortens the length of the muscle fibrils and fibres of
which they form a part, and eventually causes the entire
muscle to **contract**.

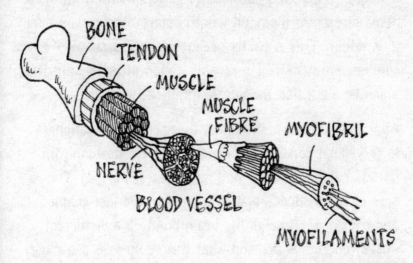

BONE
TENDON
MUSCLE
MUSCLE FIBRE
MYOFIBRIL
NERVE
BLOOD VESSEL
MYOFILAMENTS

Not all the fibres in a muscle contract at the same time – some start and end before others. But once all (or most) of the fibres in a muscle have contracted, the muscle is as short as it can get, and has reached a state of **maximum contraction**.

But what has all that got to do with stretching?

Well, when you **stretch** a muscle, the opposite happens. The thread-like myofilaments are forced to slide apart, and the overlap between their ends decreases until only a little remains. This (eventually) lengthens the muscle fibrils, fibres and entire muscles that they lie within.

But, once again, the fibres don't all lengthen out at once. Some stretch to their full length before others even begin to lengthen. This is partly because each muscle also contains special stretch-sensors called **muscle spindles**, which lie alongside the fibres within each muscle.

As the spindles are stretched, they send information to the spinal cord and brain, telling them how long the muscle has become (or how far it has stretched). This is part of the feedback system we met in the last chapter, and part of what helps the brain build up a picture of where your limbs are and what they're up to – otherwise known as **proprioception**.

So why can't you just, you know, stretch your legs into a split all in one go?

Because if a muscle is stretched too far, or too quickly, then the muscle spindles within them send a different signal to the spinal cord. This triggers a stretch reflex, as the spinal cord sends a signal back to the overstretched muscle fibres, telling them to contract. This done, the fibres tighten up and resist any further attempts to lengthen them. From this point, trying to stretch the muscle any further will only tear and damage the fibres.

So what would happen if I tried to do a full split? Like right now?

You'd probably – ahem – tear a groin muscle.

Oooooooooooh. Won't be trying that, then.

Right. If you want to **stretch** a muscle safely and successfully, you have to do two things: carefully lengthen the muscle fibres themselves, while also lengthening the muscle spindles.

Thankfully, there are lots of ways of stretching your muscles safely in order to gain flexibility.

Three Basic Types of Stretching to Try

1. **Static passive flexibility**
   - you hold a muscle or set of muscles in a stretched position using your bodyweight, or by having someone else stretch you. For example, from a standing position, you could lift your straight leg and put your foot up on a chair. Here, the weight of your own leg does the work of stretching your hamstring and calf muscles.

2. **Static active flexibility**
   - you stretch a muscle using only the strength or tension in the **opposing muscle** (or the muscle on the other side of the joint or limb). An example of this might be to stand straight and lift one straight leg until it forms a right angle with the other. Here, the **quadricep** muscle on the top of your thigh flexes to lift the leg, which stretches the **hamstring** muscle underneath.

3. **Finally, dynamic flexibility**
   – you make forceful movements that travel through the full range of a joint. For example, performing a swinging **high-kick**, **arm-circle**, or **walk-over back flip**.

All these work in different ways to increase your flexibility. And with the proper choice of stretching exercise you can make pretty much any part of the body as flexible as you want. So gymnasts and other athletes use a combination of all three of these to gain the flexibility they need for their sports.

One more thing – do you have to be skinny and fit to be flexible?

Nope. It doesn't matter what shape you are, or how good you are at running or swimming, anyone can become more flexible with training. Just give it a go.

'Hard work has made it easy.
That is my secret. That is why I win.'

Nadia Comăneci, Olympic gymnast, winner of five gold
medals and the first gymnast to score a perfect 10.0
in the history of the competition

Give it a go!

Exercise: gymnastic stretches
Type: isometric
Goal: flexibility

1. **Seal Stretch** – lie face-down on the floor, with your palms either side of your hips. Keeping your legs and the front of your hips on the ground, push with your palms and straighten your elbows. Keep going until your chest is vertical, and you're looking up at the ceiling. For an added challenge, swing both feet upward until your toes are pointed straight up at the ceiling. Hold for twenty to thirty seconds, then slowly lower yourself back to the floor.
   Stretches: lower back, hips.

2. **Cat Stretch** – now come to your hands and knees, palms flat on the floor beneath your shoulders, and toes pointed backwards, so that your shins are flat on the ground. Keeping your palms in place, rock your hips backwards until you are sitting on your heels. Your arms should be extended outward, pressed to your ears on each side. Hold for twenty to thirty seconds, then slowly rock back to all fours.
   Stretches: lower and upper back, shoulders.

3. **Palm Slide** – now sit up, legs extended out in front, and place your palms on the floor behind you, fingers pointing rearward. Keeping your arms straight, slide your hands backwards along the

floor, lowering your upper body towards the floor and stretching the shoulder area. Hold for twenty to thirty seconds, then slide back up to a seated position.

Stretches: shoulders, chest.

4. **Deep Lunge** – now stand up, placing one foot ahead of the other, and your hands on your hips. Step your forward foot out as far as you can, planting the sole of the front foot on the floor ahead of you, and the knee of the back leg on the floor behind your hips. Push your hips forward until your front and back thighs make a straight line. Hold for twenty to thirty seconds, then rock slowly and carefully back to your feet and switch sides.

Stretches: hips, quadriceps, hamstrings.

5. **Inverted Pike** – now sit down, palms on the floor beside your hips, and both legs straight out in front of you. Rock your upper body backwards, raise your knees towards your chest, rolling back until your knees are over (or, ideally, touching) your chin. Grabbing on to the backs of your ankles for support, extend your knees and straighten your legs. Point your toes, and place them on the floor above your head. Hold for twenty to thirty seconds, then let go of your ankles and slowly roll back to a seated position.

Stretches: lower back, hamstrings, calves.

Gymnastics

How do gymnasts balance on their hands?

In a perfect handstand, Olympic gymnasts look like they're standing still. But every second they spend balancing they're making lots and lots of tiny adjustments with the muscles of their hands, shoulders, stomach, back and legs, just to stay in place.

So they look like they're standing still, but actually they're moving?

In short, yes. They have to stay in constant motion – making lots of tiny pulls with muscles on every side of their bodies – just to stay upright.

So why doesn't that happen when you stand on your feet?

Actually, it does. Even when you think you're standing still, the muscles of your legs and hips are making constant, tiny adjustments too. If they didn't, you'd start toppling in less than a second.

Experiment - Balancing Act

Grab a friend, and have them stand in front of you, and place his or her hands on your shoulders.

Now have them lift their hands until their fingers and thumbs are almost (but not quite) touching the front and back of each shoulder. Their fingers should be no more than a couple of millimetres from the surface of your body.

Now stand as still as you can for two minutes, while your friend attempts to keep their hands perfectly still.

Did you keep perfectly still? It's more likely that you found yourself rebounding off your friend's fingers and thumbs. This shows you that your body, and your friend's body, are making adjustments all the time.

But why do they do that?

They have to. Since we only have two legs (rather than three, like a camera tripod, or four, like a table or chair), we have to constantly balance on them just to stay upright. It's a bit like a vertical tent pole with guy ropes attached on all sides. The ropes pull the pole in opposing directions to help keep it vertical, and without the ropes it would topple over.

But where are the ropes on a human body?

They're inside the body – in the muscles, tendons and other tissues. To stop you toppling forward, you pull with the muscle tendons and tissues of your back and the backs of your legs.

To stop you toppling backwards, you pull with the muscles and tissues at the front (or belly) side of your body – the abdominal muscles and the quadricep muscles at the front of your thighs.

There are also other muscles involved, like those of your feet, toes, hips and either side of your spine. But you get the basic idea.

143

When a gymnast is doing a handstand, a similar thing is happening, except that the hands, arms and shoulders replace the feet, legs and hips.

So why is it so much harder to stand on your hands than your feet?

For two main reasons:

1. We humans have evolved to stand on our feet. Walking on our feet, rather than our hands, allowed us to wade across rivers, to keep a lookout while moving through tall grasses, to carry things as we travelled, to wield tools, to wield weapons, and more.

2. Your body has, quite simply, had a lot more practice balancing on your feet. Depending on when you first started to stand and walk, you've been doing it since you were about one year old.

Although it can eventually become automatic balance is a **skill** and is extremely trainable.

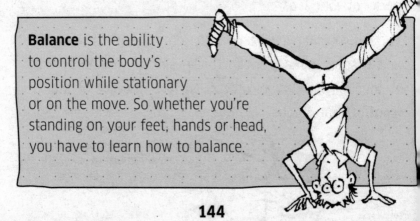

Balance is the ability to control the body's position while stationary or on the move. So whether you're standing on your feet, hands or head, you have to learn how to balance.

So how does that happen?

Balance is basically all about two things: sensing which way is down, and sensing exactly where your muscles are in 3D space.

Your most important balance-sensing organs lie deep within your ears. Just beside the snail-like cochlea of the inner ear,

you'll find the **vestibular organs** – a set of three fluid-filled organs that detect the pull of gravity (along with spinning or rotating motions of your head). In short, these organs tell you which way up you are at all times, even with your eyes closed.

Your sense of balance also makes use of the special muscle-sensing **proprioceptive** system of the body, combining information from the muscle spindles – plus other stretch-sensors within the tendons – to figure out how your arms, limbs, head and body are positioned.

In the brain, signals from the muscles, tendons, ears and eyes are combined to create your complete sense – and skill – of balance.

First Steps

As a baby, you used your sense of balance naturally to learn simple balancing skills.

- First, you learned how to sit up (i.e. balance on your bottom) without toppling over.

- Later, you learned how to stand on your feet while holding on to something (like a table, or a parent's hand) for support.

- Next, you learned to let go and balance on two feet unsupported.

- Later yet, you learned to balance on one foot at a time, and translated that into walking and running.

As with any skill, balancing takes a lot of effort and concentration at first. But after a while balance becomes automatic – part of your on-board **muscle memory**, stored in a part of the brain called the **cerebellum**.

This goes for simple balancing skills like standing on one leg, and for more complex ones like walking backwards on a balance beam.

Do all gymnasts need a good sense of balance?

Absolutely. It would be impossible to make graceful, balanced movements across a mat or beam without it. In the **pommel horse** and **parallel bars** events, male gymnasts are balancing on their hands throughout the entire, leg-swinging routine. And even in the rings, vault and high-bar events, gymnasts have to keep perfect balance upon landing, or they lose points.

RIGHT ✓   WRONG X

Get It Sorted – Point Scoring

In **floor** events, gymnasts perform acrobatic balancing and tumbling routines featuring specific moves such as rolls, handsprings, cartwheels, back-flips and somersaults. They are scored for the **difficulty**, **precision** and **beauty** of their moves across the whole floor routine.

In **vault** events, gymnasts get points for the **take-off**, **mid-air** and **landing** phases of the vault.

On the **rings**, **bars** and **pommel horse**, gymnasts are scored on the **precision** and **beauty** of specific swings and balance positions, on the move used to **dismount** the apparatus, and on the **landing** itself.

In **rhythmic gymnastics**, individuals and teams are scored not only on **precision** and **beauty**, but also the **fluidity** and grace of their movements. When using objects like the **ball**, **rope** or **ribbon**, the gymnast must keep the prop in **constant motion** throughout their routine, or face a penalty (and lost points) from the judges.

Does anyone ever get a perfect score?

It has happened, but it's very rare. One of the first to score a full set of perfect 10 scores was fourteen-year-old Romanian gymnast **Nadia Comăneci**, in the Olympic Games of 1976. She's still remembered for this today.

She was only fourteen? How did she manage that?

For one thing, she started gymnastics when she was four years old. She was doing cartwheels and balances while most other kids were busy learning how to finger-paint.

Wow. But you know what would've been really impressive . . .

What's that?

If she'd been doing cartwheels while finger-painting. Now that I'd like to see. That should totally be a new gymnastic event.

If you say so . . .

Give it a go!

Exercise: headstands and handstands
Type: static balance
Goal: improve your sense of balance!

1. **Crow Balance** - kneel on the floor, placing your palms next to your knees, fingers apart, and elbows pointing outward. Place the top of your head on the floor a little way ahead of you (if you're on a hard floor, you might want to use a cushion or folded cloth for padding), so that your head and hands form a perfect even-sided (equilateral) triangle. Both elbows should be bent, your upper arms parallel to the floor. Now shift your weight towards your head until your weight is evenly spread between your head and hands. Now lift one knee, and place it on the back of your bent elbow. Now do the same with the other knee. Hold balance for ten to twenty seconds. Try to work up to a full minute!

2. **Headstand** - kneel on the floor, 40–50cm from a wall. Repeat the steps above to get into a crow balance, with both knees propped up on your elbows. Now try extending your legs towards the ceiling, toes first. If you overbalance and your heels touch the wall, don't worry – just push gently off

and try to get your legs back to a vertical position. Hold the headstand for ten to twenty seconds. Again, try to work up to a full minute. Once you've done that, try doing the headstand away from the wall for ten to twenty seconds. Then work up to doing an unsupported headstand for a full minute.

3. **Supported Handstand** – once you've mastered the unsupported headstand, you can try the supported handstand. Stand facing a wall, bend forward and place your hands on the floor 10cm or so from the wall, shoulder-width apart. Keep your arms straight and elbows locked. Now kick your legs up – swinging one straight leg up and over your head while pushing off the floor with the opposite foot. Once both legs are vertical, and your heels are against the wall, hold the position for ten to twenty seconds. Gradually (going for ten more seconds each day), work up to balancing for a full minute against the wall. If you can do that, it's time to join a gymnastics club and learn how to handspring and backflip!

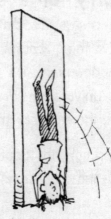

Snowboarding

Why do snowboarders stand sideways?

Standing sideways on a snowboard
helps to spread your feet and lower
your centre of mass or
centre of gravity. This
in turn makes you more
stable and balanced as you
ride. Standing sideways also helps
snowboarders to tilt and turn their
boards.

How can you lower your centre of gravity? Isn't the Earth the centre of gravity for everyone?

In some ways, yes. But only because the Earth is the most
massive thing around. Gravity isn't just a force that pulls
things downward. It's a force that attracts every object
in the universe to everything else. The more massive the
object, the stronger the force of its gravitational pull.

Quite simply, the Earth's **centre of mass** (its dense
nickel-and-iron **core**) attracts your body's centre of mass.

Where's that, then?

It's the point where the weight of the top and bottom
halves of the body are balanced out. Imagine your body
as a see-saw – with your heavy head, arms and trunk
on one side, and the heavy
bones and muscles of your
legs on the other. For most
people, the point where these
two sides balance out is found
somewhere between the hips
and the belly-button. This is
the body's own centre of mass.

When you're sitting or lying on the ground,
your centre of mass is as close to the Earth
as it can possibly get, and there's little
or no need to balance yourself (i.e. make
adjustments with your muscles, as we saw
in the last section) to stay in place.
But the higher you lift your centre of
mass – and the narrower the base it
balances on – the greater the need for
your balancing muscles, and the less
stable your body becomes.

*You can find your
own centre of gravity
by trying the 'V-sit'
exercise on page 155.*

This is why standing up straight makes you less stable (or more wobbly) than crouching. When you crouch, knees bent, your centre of mass (or belly-button) is lower to the ground.

This is also why balancing on one foot leaves you less stable than standing on two. When you stand on one foot, your body is balanced on a base less than 15cm wide. But when you stand on two feet about hip-width apart, the base supporting your weight is at least double that width, at around 30cm.

Give it a go!

Exercise: V-sit
Type: static balance
Goal: improve core muscle strength and sense of balance

1. Lie flat on the floor, legs straight, arms by your sides.

2. Keeping your back straight, raise your upper body 45º off the floor, letting your arms and hands dangle by your sides.

3. Keeping your legs straight and your knees together, now raise both legs 45º off the floor too. Try to find your 'sit bones' – the hip surfaces at the base of your gluteus maximus (bottom) muscles on which you can balance out the weight of your upper body and legs, like a see-saw.

4. Hold for thirty seconds.

5. Try to work up to a full minute.

6. For an added challenge, try walking forward (and backwards) on your bottom, keeping your legs, hands and upper body off the ground! Go for ten to twenty 'steps' in each direction. This may look a bit weird, but it's a great exercise for strength and balance!

So is that what snowboarders do?

By standing with their feet wide apart, and bending their knees to lower their centre of mass, snowboarders actually do both. The wide stance widens their base of balance, while the bent knees lowers their centre of mass. This makes it much easier for them to stay on their boards as they speed down snowy slopes.

Standing sideways also helps them to steer their boards more easily.

So how do you steer a snowboard?

The snowboarder tilts the board from side to side by leaning harder on the heels or toes. As the board tilts, the edges of the board dig in to the snow, creating friction that drags the nose (or tip) of the board from side to side.

OUCH!

In a fast turn, snowboarders tilt not just their feet, but their entire bodies back and forth to drag the board into a turn. Add to this the fact that you're hurtling downhill over a bumpy, uneven surface, and you can see why learning to snowboard involves a lot of time spent falling on your bottom.

Snowboarding Events

Downhill, slalom and giant slalom snowboarding events are played and scored in much the same way as their counterparts in skiing, with the exception of four-cross racing, in which up to four athletes race downhill over a course filled with bumps, jumps and obstacles.

Freestyle snowboarding takes place in an extended, snow-covered **half-pipe ramp**, similar to those used in skateboarding, only far longer and angled downhill so that boarders can build up speed as they traverse it. As they slide up the vertical walls of the ramp and fly into the air, the boarders perform tricks at each turn, working their way down the half-pipe in a series of spectacular spins, flips and aerial manoeuvres. To pull these tricks off successfully, freestyle snowboarders have to shift their whole bodies (and boards) around their centre of mass as they fly and flip through the air. This, as you may imagine, takes a lot of practice.

Skateboarding and surfing are two other sports where you stand sideways on your board.

Snowboarding Tricks

Board grabs   (grabbing the board with one hand in mid-air)

180° spins   (landed with the boarder riding forward)

360° spins   (landed with the boarder riding backwards)

Diving

How many somersaults can a high-diver do?

That depends how high the diving platform is, and whether the diver wants to slip gracefully into the water at the end of it, or just 'bomb it'. In theory, a diver leaping from a 10m platform could pull five or more somersaults in a row before hitting the water. But, in practice, divers rarely go for more than three.

Why not? Wouldn't they get more points for more somersaults?

Probably not. While diving judges do score dives for difficulty, they also score them for other things too. Turn the page to find out what . . .

Get It Sorted – How to Score Points in Diving Competitions

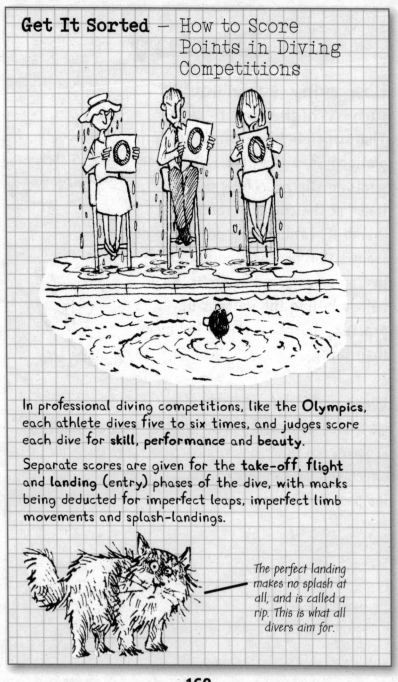

In professional diving competitions, like the **Olympics**, each athlete dives five to six times, and judges score each dive for **skill**, **performance** and **beauty**.

Separate scores are given for the **take-off**, **flight** and **landing** (entry) phases of the dive, with marks being deducted for imperfect leaps, imperfect limb movements and splash-landings.

The perfect landing makes no splash at all, and is called a rip. This is what all divers aim for.

The judges then multiply this by another number which depends on the **difficulty** of the dive to get the final score. A two-and-a-half forward somersault with twist, for example, would be multiplied by a larger number than a single forward somersault with tuck.

Judges also look at the **shape** your body makes during a dive. In diving, the three basic positions are:

Straight - the whole body is stiff and straight from neck to toe-tips.

Tuck - the body is balled up, holding the knees to the chest.

Pike - the body is bent forward, legs straight, with elbows round knees.

How and **when** the divers enter and emerge from these positions during the dive will decide most of their score.

Usually, it's the divers who made the cleanest, most beautiful-looking dives that win, rather than the ones who pulled the highest number of somersaults.

So how do divers stop somersaulting and twisting once they've started?

What d'you mean?

OK – let's say you want to do two–and–a–half somersaults with a single twist. How do you stop there, and avoid spinning on into extra twists and somersaults?

Good question. In fact, divers mostly do this with the movement of their arms while they're in the air.

When a diver wants to start a somersault, he or she does what is called a '**throw**'. To begin a **forward somersault**, you raise your arms above your head and throw your elbows down and to the front. This motion carries your upper body forward, and starts the somersault. From there, **tucking** (or curling your knees to your chest) increases your rotation speed, while pulling your body out straight will decrease it.

What if you want to do a backwards somersault instead?

To begin a **backwards somersault**, you start with a **reverse throw**. This involves crouching down a little, and lowering your arms to your sides, then throwing your hands and elbows back, up, and over your shoulders as you straighten up. This motion carries your upper body rotating backwards.

By throwing, tucking and straightening at precisely the right times, a diver can start or stop rotating at will, and control how many somersaults he or she performs.

What about twists? How do you start and stop those?

By throwing one arm up, and the other arm down, like this:

This arm motion starts the upper body twisting, and the hips and legs soon follow. By bending the elbows, the diver can speed up the twist, and by straightening the elbows, the diver slows it down.

The good news is that if you can master these movements you'll be a whizz at other sports too, such as **trampolining**, **gymnastic vault**, and **skydiving**. Even **synchronized swimmers** use similar techniques and motions to flip and twist underwater.

Really? You can do underwater somersaults?
Absolutely.

How does that work?
Well, positioning your arms and tucking your body works in the water too. So synchro swimmers use these methods to help rotate and twist themselves into position. But rather than 'throw' themselves into manoeuvres, synchro athletes push and tread at the water with their arms and legs.

In fact, the first thing you learn as a synchro swimmer is how to move or hold your position in the water with the legs alone, using water-treading **eggbeater kicks**. Next you learn **sculling**, or manoeuvring and treading water with the hands and arms. Then you combine the two, and start exploring how to twist, flip and somersault like underwater trampolinists.

Once a whole team has mastered these moves, they can then arrange themselves into patterns to perform specific moves and routines. This is where the real fun begins.

There are a limited number of recognized 'move' types in synchro. The basic moves include:

Platform lifts – one swimmer is raised and held clear of the water by the others, who float beneath the surface.

Stacked lifts – one or more swimmers stand on the shoulders of the others, with both lifters and liftees raised above the surface.

Throws – one or more swimmers are thrown clear of the surface by the others, clearing the surface completely like a breaching dolphin before landing gracefully back in the water.

You get to throw each other about in the pool?

Yep.

Smart! I usually get thrown out by a lifeguard when I start doing that kind of thing . . .

Next time, just keep it graceful, and tell him you're practising for the Olympics.

Nahh. That won't work.

Why not?

I already tried that with the snorkel, remember?

Oh, yeah. So you did.

Give it a go!

Exercise: synchro flips

Type: skill

Goal: improve dexterity and agility in the water

Pike Flip

1. Begin by treading water, feet down, your head above the surface.

2. While scooping water upward and forward with both hands, dive your head forward and underwater, pointing the top of your head to the bottom.

3. Keeping both legs straight and your feet together, let your hips rise out of the water until the backs of your legs are level with the surface.

4. Keep scooping (sculling) the water towards your face, rotating your head right under as your hips dip below the surface.

5. Bend your knees towards your chest, then scoop water behind you with both hands to stop your head from popping up too quickly.

6. Finally, extend your feet towards the bottom, and wait for rapturous applause.

Back Flips

1. Begin by lying flat out on the surface, face up.

2. Scoop your arms out to your sides underwater, then force yourself backwards and underwater by pushing your hands overhead.

3. Tuck your knees to your chest and make yourself into the smallest ball possible.
4. Flip yourself over backwards by pushing the water over your head.
5. Bring your knees right over your head and towards the bottom of the pool.
6. Extend both feet towards the bottom and surface for applause, or tip backwards and go for another one!

Index

Thanks to . . .

Gaby Morgan, Steph Woolley and all at Macmillan Children's Books for their help, advice and continued support.

Holly Cave, Deborah Patterson and everyone at the Science Museum who offered comments and suggestions.

Dr David G. Haase, Professor of Physics at NC State University, for generously offering his help, suggestions and reference material.

Jennifer Jackson Weston at NC State University, for (once again) setting me up with the experts, and for very graciously ignoring a visit from President Obama to have lunch with me instead :o)

My brilliant sister (and fellow author) Lorna Murphy, whose Skype chats helped keep me sane.

Aaron Marco, whose physical therapy sessions helped keep me in one piece.

Brandon Sommerfeld, Martin Wheeler, Kwan Lee and Mark Jakabcsin – who all did their best to take me apart again.

Russ Campbell, Minou Pham and Scot Schwichow – all Olympians in their own way.

Chris, Susie, Heather, Sean and the Fuzzball – big luv to you all.

And, most of all, my parents, Frank and Josephine Murphy – still sporty at well past sixty, and my daily inspiration to do better.

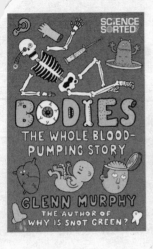

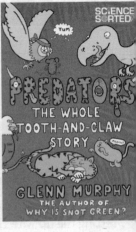

Collect them all!